IMAGES
of America

SYRACUSE POLICE

ON THE COVER. Members of the Syracuse Police Department, under the command of Sgt. John Delahanty, are photographed in front of the State Armory on West Jefferson Street during the Municipal Day celebration on June 17, 1915. (Courtesy of Syracuse Police Archives.)

IMAGES
of America

SYRACUSE POLICE

Daniel F. Walsh, Thomas L. Derby,
and Russell W. Gates
Foreword by Chief Frank L. Fowler

ARCADIA
PUBLISHING

ISBN 978-0-7385-7654-1

Published by Arcadia Publishing
Charleston, South Carolina

Printed in the United States of America

Library of Congress Control Number: 2011929910

For all general information, please contact Arcadia Publishing:
Telephone 843-853-2070
Fax 843-853-0044
E-mail sales@arcadiapublishing.com
For customer service and orders:
Toll-Free 1-888-313-2665

Visit us on the Internet at www.arcadiapublishing.com

To the Syracuse police officers who have lived this history and to their loved ones who have shared the burdens and sacrifices.

Contents

FOREWORD

For the last two years, I have had the honor of serving as chief of the Syracuse Police Department. Ours is an organization rich in honor, tradition, and history. For 163 years, men and women have preserved peace and fought crime on the streets of the city, and they have built a police department to be proud of.

The pages that follow will introduce you to some of those men and women. The images will reflect some of their sacrifices and achievements. They will provide a glimpse at some of their personalities and emotions. For some, they will be a reminiscence of people and times gone by; for others, an introduction to a police department richer in heritage than they knew existed. Most importantly, I hope that they will tell some the story of the Syracuse Police Department.

—Chief Frank L. Fowler

ACKNOWLEDGEMENTS

The authors would like to thank the many active and retired members of the Syracuse Police Department and their families who have contributed to this book. Without their photographs and historical knowledge, it would not have been possible. We would like to specifically thank Chief Frank L. Fowler for his appreciation of this police department's history and his support in this project. Most importantly, we thank the men and women who have built this history and those who will carry it on and write the pages of the future.

INTRODUCTION

Today, approximately 500 men and women provide police service for the City of Syracuse. Officers receive state-of-the-art training and equipment. Computer and communications technologies now permit them to learn of, respond to, and investigate crime faster and more efficiently than ever before. Such was not always the case, though.

Syracuse began as an uninviting swamp in central New York. Following the discovery of its salt springs, however, the area took on a new appeal. Salt producers began to settle in the area, and with them came an industry that until 1900 produced most of the salt used in the United States. By 1825, village officers were elected, and the Village of Syracuse was born. Another major development occurred in 1825 with the opening of the Erie Canal. The canal joined the Atlantic Ocean with the Great Lakes, and Syracuse's salt industry boomed with the increased ease of transportation. Shippers and travelers found their way to Syracuse, and the population grew rapidly.

It soon became clear to villagers that the protection afforded to them by the constables of the day was insufficient. A petition authored by Ambrose Kasson was presented "for the purpose of suppressing vice and immorality in this village." On September 13, 1826, the trustees responded by appointing A. Northam and H. Young to provide a house or room that would be designated as a watch house. They further resolved that a fund would be raised through contributions from the community that would permit "trustees to organize and keep on foot for one month a Village Watch to consist of not less than four persons."

A constabulary was formed under Henry W. Durnford to address the problems of the roustabouts, gamblers, and denizens of "robbers roosts" along lower James Street that mingled with and preyed upon the canal and warehouse workers. Records indicate that in March 1827, Durnford's salary was $25 for the year. The following year, Durnford received some assistance when Charles Cook performed similar duties for the same pay.

As the village continued to grow, so too did the need for additional policing. On January 8, 1828, the village trustees, in an effort to clean up the streets, prohibited "all gaming, raffling or playing of cards or dice" in "Grocery Shops, or Cellars, including Houses, or other Shops, which are licensed for the retailing of spirituous liquors to be drank therein."

Policing of the village was intermittent, and often, additional or "special" constables and policemen were appointed to address temporary conditions, such as celebrations, horse races, and rashes of arson. July 4, 1838, for example, signaled the need for additional police presence. In response, on July 2 of that year, six men were appointed to a night watch. They would perform their duties for six nights, for a dollar per night. With the passing of the holiday, the watch was cut in half, and on July 16, the remaining watchmen were dismissed. In 1841, several events and decisions occurred that helped to shape the police service in Syracuse. First, on January 13, a resolution was passed that called for a committee consisting of the trustees and three other individuals to make amendments to the charter "that will give the village a more vigorous police." Then in

May, came another resolution calling for the appointment of a regular police justice who was to be selected in the same manner as county court judges. On August 21, 1841, the Goings shop was the site of a fire and subsequent gunpowder explosion; 26 people were killed and 64 injured. The public outcry was deafening in its suggestion that arson was the cause. On August 26, citing "a large number of gamblers and evil disposed persons" in their midst, the trustees announced that a public meeting would be held to address the matters at hand. That meeting took place on August 28, and so many villagers turned out that the gathering had to be moved to a larger venue. They called for the trustees to appoint three additional constables. It was reported that there were 75 establishments where liquor was sold in the village. The committee concluded that the condition required "extraordinary measures to protect citizens and their property." The committee also cited the presence of gaming houses, horse races scheduled for the following September, and a large number of fires, many suspicious in origin, as reasons for additional police coverage.

On September 3, to address the conditions, $600, the largest sum ever allotted for public safety by the village, was raised to provide another night watch. On September 6, Henry Gifford, William A. Cook, and Russel Hebbard were appointed village constables. The following day, night watchmen Nathan W. Rose, Joseph Flick, Joseph Mesmer, James Burrell, Charles Huntoon, and Thomas Griffith were appointed. Rose served as captain of the night watch, and each man received a dollar per night for his service, with Nathan Rose receiving an additional 50¢ per night. The watch served until early December of that year. Zophar H. Adams, Philo N. Rust, and Joseph Flick were also pressed into temporary service in 1841 as special police constables to provide additional protection during the Fourth of July celebration.

Police service in Syracuse continued to be sporadic and reactionary for several more years. Then, on New Year's Eve 1846, Syracusans gathered to celebrate at Sigel's Coffee House at South Warren and Washington Streets. A contingent of salt boilers from the neighboring village of Salina had the same idea, and long-standing rivalries escalated into what became known as the Coffee House Riot. Once again, the inadequacy of the police service reared its head, and it was necessary to call in a militia unit, drilling locally to quell the riot. When the gun smoke cleared and the blood dried, the people had had enough. The villages of Syracuse and Salina joined. In 1848, the City of Syracuse was born, and with this, began the story of the Syracuse Police Department.

Syracuse Police will introduce most of you to some of the police officers who have helped to build the police department into a nationally recognized law enforcement organization. For others who have lived the moments or known the people, this will be a walk down memory lane. In the images, you will see virtually every human emotion imaginable and some that you probably could not have imagined. You will see Syracuse police officers behind the scenes, in moments generally shared only among themselves. The photographs that you are about to view have been taken from dusty trunks, mantels, and the treasure chests of old cops and the people who love them—and generously shared for your enjoyment. They will evoke entertainment, sadness, quiet recollections, and remember-when conversations.

The authors have drawn upon years of experience and research to produce this book. Det. Daniel F. Walsh is a six-year veteran assigned to the Criminal Investigation Division (CID). Sgt. Thomas L. Derby, also assigned to CID, is a 20-year veteran. Lt. Russell W. Gates, a 34-year law enforcement veteran, was designated department historian by Chief James T. Foote, and he is assigned to the Patrol Division. Together, they invite you to share the experience as they introduce you to the Syracuse Police.

During the centennial celebration of the Syracuse City Hall in September 1989, police officer Rod Carr (right) shows Mayor Thomas Young a chain come-along, or "nippers." Also visible on the table is a cap belonging to patrolman James Hannon, who was killed in the line of duty in 1929. A rare copy of Chief William "Pop" O'Brien's book *Forty Years on the Force* can also be seen standing on the far-right side of the table. (Courtesy of Syracuse Police Archives.)

One

Chiefs

A total of 30 men have held the title of chief of police for the City of Syracuse. Chief Frank L. Fowler accepted that responsibility in January 2010, and today, he maintains the delicate balance between providing courteous and attentive service to the community while ensuring that the officers delivering that service are properly equipped and safe in an increasingly dangerous world. (Courtesy of Syracuse Police Archives.)

James Harvey served as chief of police for only a short time between 1880 and 1881. It was a highly political time in Syracuse, and there was turmoil between saloon owners and temperance people. The conditions led to his removal. Additionally, Chief Harvey's own personality may have played a significant role in his departure. Harvey was brought before the commissioners to answer several charges, including complaints from a faction of the force worried about the chief's abrasiveness and gruff demeanor. The commissioners ultimately concluded that Chief Harvey would be dismissed for the good of the force. It is important, however, to bear in mind that the city functioned under a ward system, and appointments to the police force were based on political affiliations. James Harvey returned to the police department a short time later when the political winds changed. He was appointed as a detective and held that position until he was murdered, making him the first Syracuse police officer killed in the line of duty. Interestingly, at the time of his death, Harvey was referred to as one of the most respected members of the force. (Courtesy of Syracuse Police Archives.)

Charles Rial Wright had a newspaper and theatrical background. He worked as sports editor for the *Syracuse Courier* and then as business manager for the Grand Opera House before he reluctantly accepted an appointment as chief of police. Wright began his long tenure by calling together his 30 men and informing them of his personal policy—"Be all ears and no mouth"—and encouraging them to do the same. (Courtesy of Syracuse Police Archives.)

Martin L. Cadin was a New York State assemblyman in May 1905 when Mayor Ralph Bowen met him in Albany and asked him to replace Charles Wright as chief. Cadin agreed, but the law prevented him from holding two offices, and his term did not expire until the end of the year. So, Cadin took a desk at police headquarters and learned the job without pay while he finished his term. (Courtesy of Syracuse Police Archives.)

When Chief Cadin was officially appointed on New Years Day, 100 friends appeared in his office and presented him with a gold badge that held a two-and-a-half-karat diamond. Throughout his career as chief, Cadin enjoyed the admiration of residents and policemen alike. These photographs show department members assembled on the steps of the Onondaga County Courthouse to commemorate the appointment of Martin Cadin as chief of police. Those identified are, from left to right, (first row) Capt. Tom Quigley, Lt. Jacob Warner, Capt. Peter Neumann, Sgt. August Decker, Deputy Chief William O'Brien, Chief Martin L. Cadin, Sgt. August Eabold, Sgt. John Fay, Det. Sgt. James Shepard, and Sgt. John Cummings. (Courtesy of Syracuse Police Archives.)

Patrolmen John Forsythe (left) and Paul Wolford (right) are congratulated by Chief Martin Cadin (center) during Municipal Day ceremonies on July 6, 1931. Forsythe received the Hendricks Medal for his arrest of a suspect in a shooting at the Elk Hotel in East Syracuse on December 8, 1930. Wolford received the Herald Medal for his capture of three safecrackers at the Progressive Laundry at West Taylor and Onieda Streets on June 19, 1930. (Courtesy of Syracuse Police Archives.)

Thomas Carroll was deputy chief in May 1934 when Mayor Rolland Marvin suspended Chief Cadin following a disagreement. The mayor put Carroll in charge over First Deputy Chief George Peacock. Cadin was returned to duty three days later, but he retired by the end of the year. Once again, Carroll was appointed over Peacock. He held the position until his death in 1937. (Courtesy of Syracuse Police Archives.)

George S. Peacock served as a deputy chief for 16 years under three chiefs before he was finally made acting chief on July 30, 1937. Though he only held the position for five months, he is remembered for directing the manhunt for escaped kidnappers John Oley, Percy Geary, and Harold Crowley. Federal, state, county, and city police scoured the city, capturing them within three days without a single shot fired. (Courtesy of Syracuse Police Archives.)

William E. Rapp was public safety commissioner when he was appointed as chief. Under his command, two-way radios were installed in patrol cars and he created a juvenile delinquency unit. During his regime, Rapp was also credited for an outstanding crime clearance rate and dramatically reducing the number of traffic accidents. (Courtesy of Syracuse Police Archives.)

John A. Kinney seemed destined for advancement from the time of his appointment as a patrolman on December 30, 1913. He spent his first three years on special assignment to the mayor. He spent another two years assigned to the Health Department, and on May 1, 1928, he was promoted to lieutenant and instructor and tasked with starting the police school. During his time as chief, the department was widely recognized for its traffic safety accomplishments and a crime rate in his final year that was 25 percent lower than comparable Mid-Atlantic cities. (Courtesy of Syracuse Police Archives.)

Frederick G. Arnold was sworn in as chief on October 8, 1954. Mayor Mead gave him marching orders to revamp the department and restore public confidence in it. Among the priorities for him to address were to instill better discipline and improve the level of courtesy to the public. While Arnold began to institute changes, within six months of his appointment, he was forced to retire because of illness. (Courtesy of Syracuse Police Archives.)

Chief Fred Arnold (left) and Deputy Chief Harold Kelley (second from left) promote Samuel Nappi (third from left) to captain and Andrew Peltz (right) to lieutenant on April 9, 1955. Nappi and Peltz were both members of the Blue Ribbon Squad, a group of men who were appointed on January 1, 1942, all of whom made rank. (Courtesy of Syracuse Police Archives.)

Harold F. Kelley took office in 1955. Almost from the beginning, there were accusations of corruption in his ranks. It was alleged that detectives were providing protection for gambling operations, such as that of Percy Harris. By 1960, Mayor Walsh appointed "Super Chief" Charles Sloane to oversee Kelley's administration. Frustrated by what he perceived as a lack of commitment to clean house, Sloane resigned within a few months. In 1962, the State Crime Commission substantiated many of the allegations. Kelley had no choice but to leave. (Courtesy of Syracuse Police Archives.)

Police chief Harold Kelley (left) took time out of his schedule to meet with these two police officers from Vietnam in July 1958. (Courtesy of Syracuse Police Archives.)

Chief Kelley (left) congratulates patrolman Chester Piatkowski on winning yet another firearms trophy in October 1960. Piatkowski received the trophy for being the highest scorer of 40 participants in the FBI firearms training school at Camp Smith, Peekskill. Piatkowski took over the leadership of the police pistol team after the retirement of Sgt. Frank Lesicki. The group was a highly competitive and consistently top-rated team. (Courtesy of Syracuse Police Archives.)

Det. John Forsythe (left) is greeted by Chief Harold Kelley during the annual medals ceremony on June 20, 1958. Though Forsythe was not receiving a medal that day, it was traditional for the winners of previous Herald and Hendricks Medals to attend the festivities each year to honor the new recipients. (Courtesy of Syracuse Police Archives.)

On December 9, 1962, Mayor William F. Walsh (center) announced that the police department would be run by a commission comprised of him, Stewart F. Hancock Jr. (left), and William G. Wright (right), a former Syracuse police officer who was serving as city personnel director at the time. The dramatic action became necessary in the wake of the resignation of Chief Kelley following the State Crime Commission investigation. (Courtesy of Syracuse Police Archives.)

Following several difficult years for the police department, Mayor William Walsh reached beyond its ranks for new leadership. Inspector Patrick V. Murphy, of the New York City Police Department, took the reins while on leave from the New York department. Below, Mayor Walsh (left) can be seen below as he witnesses Chief Patrick V. Murphy (center) take the oath of office. The new chief was enthusiastic in bringing change to the department. On June 18, 1964, however, he resigned from Syracuse and returned to New York to accept a promotion to deputy chief inspector. He would later become commissioner of the New York Police Department. (Both, courtesy of Syracuse Police Archives.)

On day one, Chief Murphy made a point of meeting with as many members of the department as possible; one of his first meetings was with four of his captains. Here, he meets with, from left to right, First Platoon captain William McCarthy, Third Platoon Provisionary captain Joseph Franey, administrative captain Harold Shea, and Second Platoon captain Samuel Nappi. (Courtesy of Syracuse Police Archives.)

During his first-day tour of the Public Safety Building on January 14, 1963, Chief Murphy (left) meets with Sgt. Victor McNett, commanding officer of the crime lab. The sergeant explains current lab procedures and shows the chief some of the apparatus available to perform those procedures. (Courtesy of Syracuse Police Archives.)

On June 5, 1964, just 13 days before his resignation from the department, Chief Patrick V. Murphy (second from left in both images) meets with Lt. John C. Dillon (plainclothes), Sgt. Frank Lesicki, and patrolman Chester Piatkowski to discuss the ballistic body armor that Piatkowski is modeling. Upon close examination, it appears that the chief may be pointing to the bullet impact area on the vest. A similar area can be seen several inches beneath it. They may be the result of ballistic testing. (Both, courtesy of Syracuse Police Archives.)

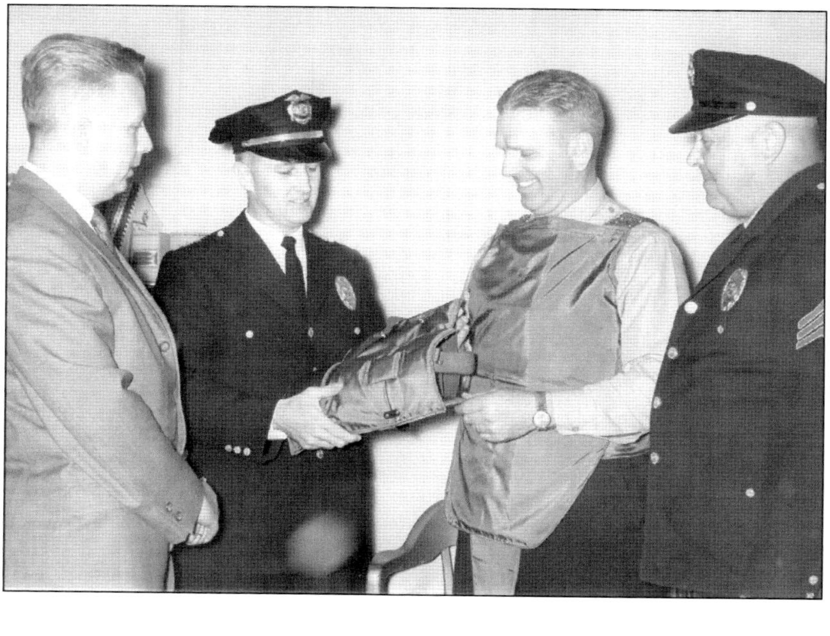

William H.T. Smith traveled from New York City with Patrick V. Murphy to be his first deputy chief. When Murphy resigned on June 18, 1964, Smith was appointed by Mayor William Walsh to take his place. Smith had more than 20 years experience with the New York City Police Department before coming to Syracuse. Upon arrival in Syracuse, Smith organized the plan to address vice in the city. (Courtesy of Syracuse Police Archives.)

The chief officers meet on the range in the basement of the Public Safety Building for firearms qualifications on October 22, 1964. On the line are, from left to right, Deputy Chief John Clark, Chief William H.T. Smith, Deputy Chief Harold Shea, Deputy Chief Samuel Nappi, and Deputy Chief John Holihan. Standing behind the line are, from left to right, patrolman Chester Piatkowski, Sgt. Frank Tysco, unidentified, Sgt. Frank Lesicki, and unidentified. (Courtesy of Syracuse Police Archives.)

Chief William H.T. Smith (center) is presented with a plaque by Police Benevolent Association officers William Judkins (left) and Robert Smith (right). The award expressed appreciation for the chief's contributions to the police department and assistance to the Police Benevolent Association. (Courtesy of Syracuse Police Archives.)

Thomas J. Sardino began his war on vice before he became a police officer. He and his two brothers took it upon themselves to stamp out vice after their father's liquor license was taken away. After he became an officer, he continued his campaign. Sardino's career with the Syracuse Police Department spanned 32 years, and for 15 of those years, he served as chief. (Courtesy of Syracuse Police Archives.)

Police officer Charles DelCostello (center) was awarded the WHEN 5 Gold Badge award on June 27, 1974. He was recognized for his overall performance in addition to his extensive civic contributions. He was a leader in the Officer Friendly program as well. Chief Thomas Sardino (right) is seen here congratulating DelCostello on his accomplishment. The other man is unidentified. (Courtesy of the family of Charles DelCostello.)

Chief Leigh Hunt (seated at the head of the conference table) is conducting a press conference regarding an arrest in the murder of a downtown prostitute. It was unknown at the time that the suspect had murdered another prostitute earlier. That would not be discovered until after the killer had served prison time and been paroled. After exhaustive investigation by the Manlius Police Department, where the body had been found, the same killer confessed and returned to prison. (Courtesy of Syracuse Police Archives.)

James T. Foody retired from the New York State Police as a major and worked as a prosecutor in Oswego County before accepting the position of chief of police in Syracuse in January 1994. During his term as chief, the murder, rape, and robbery rates fell to their lowest point in 10 years. (Courtesy of Syracuse Police Archives.)

John Falge served as chief of police from August 16, 1999, until July 11, 2001. He spent his entire law enforcement career with the Syracuse Police Department. Falge moved up through the ranks while attending law school at Syracuse University, eventually becoming a lawyer while still a serving police officer. (Courtesy of Syracuse Police Archives.)

Dennis DuVal first gained public attention when he played basketball at Syracuse University. He then spent two years in the NBA playing for the Washington Bullets and the Atlanta Hawks. DuVal then returned to Syracuse where he was appointed as a Syracuse police officer in 1978. On July 11, 2001, he was appointed as the first African American chief of police in Syracuse, a position that he held until he retired in 2004. (Courtesy of Syracuse Police Archives.)

There are currently 25 active and retired surviving Syracuse police chiefs and deputy chiefs. On June 18, 2011, a group of 12 met at Francesca's on North Salina Street for a luncheon. From left to right are chiefs Gary Miguel, Frank Fowler, Leigh Hunt, John Falge, Dennis DuVal, and Steven Thompson. (Courtesy of William Hanna.)

Two

COMMUNICATIONS

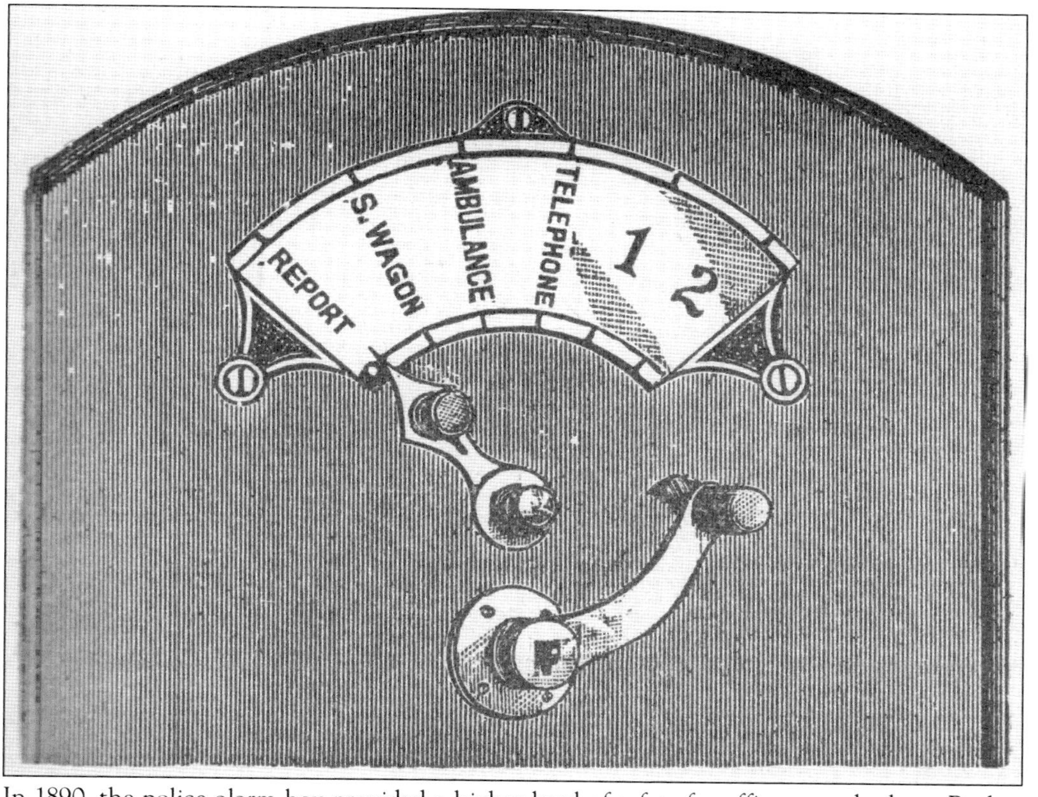

In 1890, the police alarm box provided a higher level of safety for officers on the beat. Rather than having to run blocks to a telephone to call for assistance, officers could simply go to one of the numerous call boxes and signal the station. They opened the box; turned the pointer to slow or fast (patrol) wagon, ambulance, or report; and pulled the lever to inform headquarters of their status or need. (Courtesy of Syracuse Police Archives.)

It was a simpler time in 1898 when the police department could make the search for a couple of unreturned rental bicycles this kind of a priority. Cards like this were disseminated to the community and to neighboring law enforcement agencies to alert them of stolen property, wanted parties, and general police information. (Both, courtesy of Russell Gates.)

BICYCLES STOLEN.

$10.00 REWARD. $10.00

At 2:20 and 2:30 P. M., June 28th, 1898, two young men, presumably confederates, each rented a bicycle at the Cycle Livery of H. W. Morrell, 419 South State Street, this city, for one hour, and have not returned them to date.

One **TOURIST BICYCLE,** '97 Model, No. 11,054, dark red frame, name "W. F. Butler" painted on top bar, Kensington tires, rear tire has inner tube, Tourist saddle, combination pedals, adjustable steel handle bar, cork grips.

One **RECORD BICYCLE,** '97 Model, No. 7184, maroon colored frame, Chase tires, Gordon saddle, rat trap pedals, adjustable handle bars, cork grips, dark tips. (New Wheel.)

Thief No. 1, gave the name of A. Harding, was about 23 years. 5 ft. 6 in., dark complexion. 140 pounds. Wore dark suit, and black derby hat. No. 2, gave name of C. Beck, was about 22 years, 5 ft. 7 or 8 in., 140 pounds, smooth face, dressed in dark suit and soft hat. Both gave fictitious city addresses.

A reward of $5.00 each for recovery of wheels, arrest and conviction of thieves is offered by the owner, H. W. Morrell.

Please notify pawnshops, bicycle dealers, repairers, liveries, etc. Take possession of wheels wherever found, arrest any one offering them for pawn, sale, exchange or repair, and notify,

CHAS. R. WRIGHT,
Chief of Police.

SYRACUSE, N. Y., June 29th, 1898.

This letter exemplifies some of the conflict faced by Syracuse law enforcement personnel at the time. The opposing positions of saloon owners and supporters and Anti-Saloon League and temperance people were very politically charged. Confrontations frequently escalated into disturbances in the streets and, in at least one case, played a role in the change of leadership in the police department. (Courtesy of Syracuse Police Archives.)

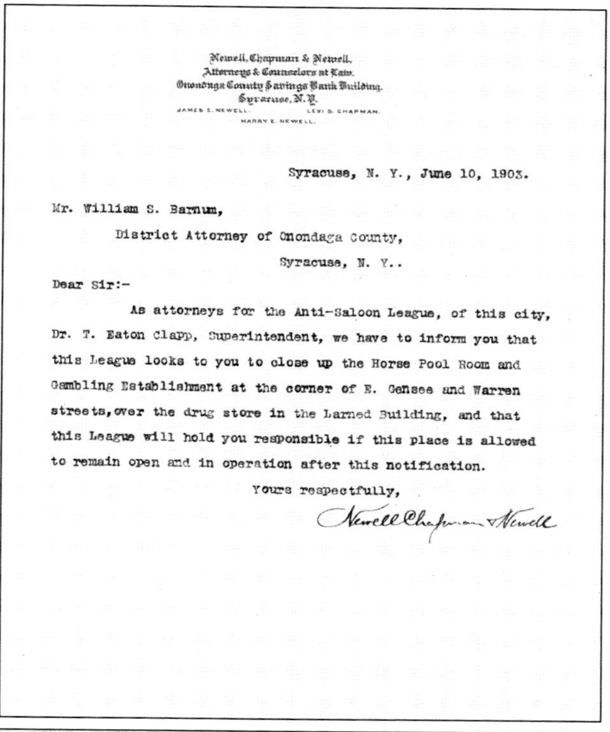

Newell, Chapman & Newell,
Attorneys & Counselors at Law.
Onondaga County Savings Bank Building.
Syracuse, N.Y.
JAMES E. NEWELL. LEVI S. CHAPMAN.
HARRY E. NEWELL.

Syracuse, N. Y., June 10, 1903.

Mr. William S. Barnum,
District Attorney of Onondaga County,
Syracuse, N. Y..

Dear Sir:-

As attorneys for the Anti-Saloon League, of this city, Dr. T. Eaton Clapp, Superintendent, we have to inform you that this League looks to you to close up the Horse Pool Room and Gambling Establishment at the corner of E. Gensee and Warren streets, over the drug store in the Larned Building, and that this League will hold you responsible if this place is allowed to remain open and in operation after this notification.

Yours respectfully,
Newell Chapman & Newell

In the days before teletypes and computers, the everyday clerical and administrative tasks and inquiries were more burdensome. What today can be handled in a matter of seconds with a simple telephone call or keystroke could take days or weeks in the past. (Courtesy of Syracuse Police Archives.)

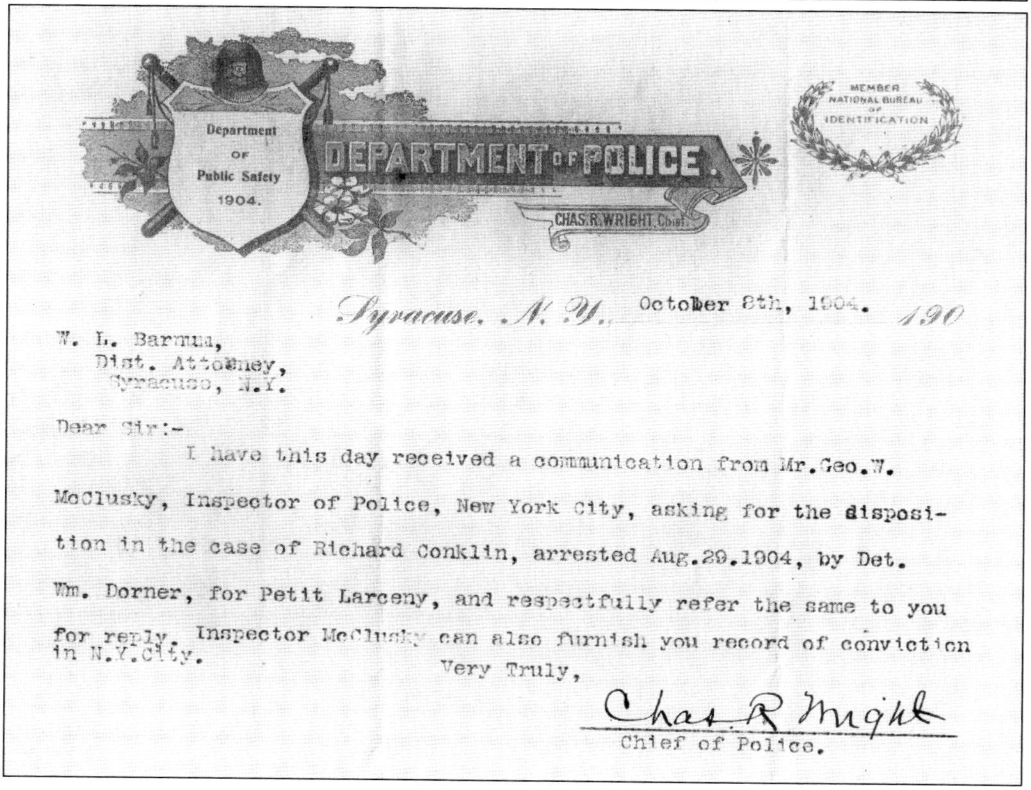

Syracuse, N. Y., October 8th, 1904.

W. L. Barnum,
Dist. Attorney,
Syracuse, N.Y.

Dear Sir:-

I have this day received a communication from Mr. Geo. W. McClusky, Inspector of Police, New York City, asking for the disposition in the case of Richard Conklin, arrested Aug. 29. 1904, by Det. Wm. Dorner, for Petit Larceny, and respectfully refer the same to you for reply. Inspector McClusky can also furnish you record of conviction in N.Y. City.

Very Truly,
Chas. R. Wright
Chief of Police.

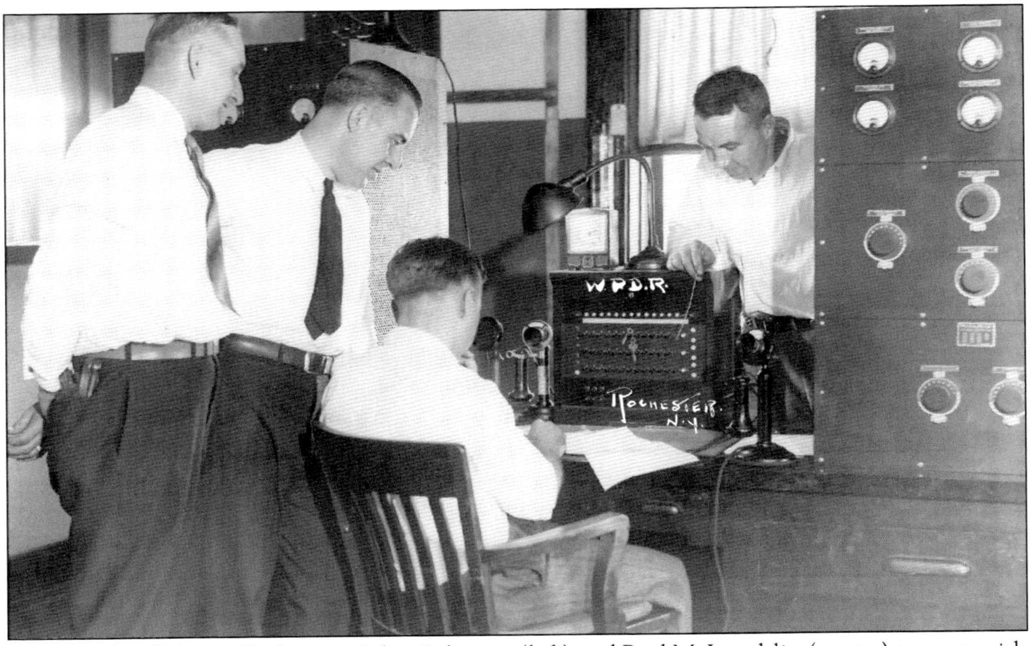

In 1931, Chief Martin Cadin sent John Arbogast (left) and Paul McLaughlin (center) to meet with William Cornell (right), of the Rochester Police Department. He would prepare them to set up the first police radio system for Syracuse. Here, they watch as an unidentified worker demonstrates the operation of Rochester PD radio station WPDR. (Courtesy of Syracuse Police Archives.)

The first radios were one-way radios. Here, William Cornell (left) shows Paul McLaughlin (center) and John Arbogast (right) the tubes and inner workings of a radio receiving unit. The pictured unit would be situated behind the front seat of a patrol car, and an officer would be positioned there to monitor any calls transmitted to them through headphones. (Courtesy of Syracuse Police Archives.)

Paul McLaughlin (left) explains the process as Chief Martin Cadin watches Sgt. Martin Nixon receive calls through the telephone switchboard and then dispatch them over the new radio system. The first home to the Syracuse Police Department radio transmitting station, WPEA, was in McChesney Park in 1931. It was later moved to the Willow Street station. (Courtesy of Syracuse Police Archives.)

By December 1931, the decision was made to centralize the entire communication system. All the equipment was moved to the top floor of the Willow Street station. In this photograph, Paul McLaughlin (left) can be seen seated at the dispatch desk; the other man is unidentified. The lighted territory map can be seen on the wall over the desk. Once surrounding agencies recognized the success of the system, Syracuse assumed dispatching duties for the Onondaga County Sheriff's Office and the New York State Police units operating locally. (Courtesy of Syracuse Police Archives.)

In this 1948 photograph, patrolmen Marvin Drew (back) and Charles Dawson (front) field calls at the police switchboard before deciding what will be dispatched. Dawson was the 1943 recipient of the Herald Medal. His fondest memories were of his 10 years as a motorcycle patrolman and sergeant. In 1976, he retired as a captain commanding the Traffic Division. (Courtesy of Syracuse Police Archives.)

This unidentified operator is entering information for a teletype message in the late 1940s. The teletype greatly increased the speed and ease with which information could be circulated. The system, though modernized, is still in use today. (Courtesy of Syracuse Police Archives.)

In January 1947, the police department began hiring civilian telephone operators in an effort to free up police officers for street duties. Esther Richards, pictured here in 1948, was one of the first civilian operators appointed. Over the years, she became known for her cheerful, "sprightly" personality. (Courtesy of Syracuse Police Archives.)

After spending about three years filling in as relief dispatcher and complaint clerk, patrolman Charles Morgan was appointed to the position of dispatcher following the retirement of Edward Geiger on November 16, 1952. (Courtesy of Syracuse Police Archives.)

Chief William H.T. Smith (left) and First Deputy Chief John Holihan (right) watch the dispatch process in the communications office in 1964. At the time, communications was located on the fourth floor of the Public Safety Building, where the chiefs complex is now located. (Courtesy of Syracuse Police Archives.)

This unidentified police officer is prioritizing the complaint cards that have been relayed to him before dispatching the information. (Courtesy of Syracuse Police Archives.)

Three

TRANSPORTATION

Syracuse has used many methods to patrol the city. In 1885, they used a horse-drawn patrol wagon to deploy officers throughout the city. In 1905, the first police car hit the streets. Officers were assigned to patrol on horses and catch speeding cars on motorcycles in 1909. The one patrol method that has remained constant from the beginning is the cop on the beat. This unidentified officer walked his beat on the city's north side. (Courtesy of Syracuse Police Archives.)

Police officers Mark Rathbun (left) and John Mulherin (right) walk their beat on South Avenue in the early 1980s. Located at the foot of St. Agnes Hill, which can be seen in the background, is the Elmwood section of the city. It was once a separate village with its own police department until annexed by the city around 1900. (Courtesy of Syracuse Police Archives.)

The Team Oriented Policing (TOP) Unit relied heavily on foot patrols when it was created to target high-incident areas in the city. Working out of an office trailer in the target area, TOP officers assessed the issues and needs of the area through direct and ongoing contact with residents and business owners and tailored their methods to address them. Officers Russell Gates (left) and Tracy Johnson (right) walk Catherine Street in this 1992 photograph. (Courtesy of the *Post Standard*.)

The first patrol wagon rolled through the streets of Syracuse on October 13, 1885. The bottle-green wagon was built by the Cortland Omnibus Company. The wagon carried officers to remote assignments, emergency calls, and performed ambulance duties. Stretchers were carried under the seats on each side of the wagon bed. Handcuffs and medicine were carried in a cabinet under the driver's seat. (Courtesy of Syracuse Police Archives.)

This electric patrol wagon, manufactured by the Electric Vehicle Company of Hartford, Connecticut, was put into operation July 1, 1905. It carried 12 passengers and traveled at a top speed of 18 miles an hour. It cost a third less to operate than the horse-drawn wagon. The vehicle was stored at the Amos-Pierce Company on South State Street until the police horse barn was converted for that purpose. (Courtesy Syracuse Police Archives.)

The newly formed Mounted Traffic Squad was assigned to handle traffic and crowd control for the New York State Fair in September 1909. From left to right are patrolmen Michael McCarthy, Leroy Hepp, Edward Bamrick, August Maurer, Thomas Cahill, Ernest Digney, George Peacock, David Brilbeck, Frank Candee, George Wickens, Jake Letterman, Henry Brazell, and Thomas Atkinson. (Courtesy of Russell Gates.)

Mounted units have come and gone in the Syracuse Police Department in much the same way as motorcycles have. They have been used for traffic control, crowd control, and park patrol. Mounted officers carry the colors in the photograph above, which was taken in the early 1950s. The increase of vehicular traffic over the years has somewhat diminished the role horses play in traffic control. (Courtesy of Lt. Jonathan Anderson.)

Mounted police officer Daniel Corbett is seen riding his horse along a city street in the 1990s, as Sgt. David Fixx watches traffic. Officer Corbett would later be forced to retire as the result of an injury he sustained working with his horse. (Courtesy of Syracuse Police Archives.)

Chief of police Leigh Hunt is seen seated on a police department mount in this 1986 photograph. The picture was taken in front of the Mounted Section stables at the New York State Fairgrounds. Standing before the chief are, from left to right, Sgt. Vincent Quatrone and police officers Ray Starner, Geoff Fahringer, and David Sackett. (Courtesy of Syracuse Police Archives.)

The horses of the Mounted Section were always a popular attraction with children and adults alike wherever they went. They proved to be a tremendous asset to police-community relations in addition to being effective enforcement partners for their riders. Police officer Kevin Bastedo is seen letting some citizens get acquainted with his horse. Bastedo retired several years later as a sergeant. (Courtesy of Syracuse Police Archives.)

By the late 1980s, the Mounted Section's time was coming to an end. Perhaps the issue most responsible for it being disbanded in 1990 was the number of officers who sustained long-term injuries. Shown performing ceremonial duties are, from left to right, Sgt. Kenneth Southwell and police officers David Ware, Walter Peczyinski, and Maureen Buckland. (Courtesy of Syracuse Police Archives.)

Motorcycle patrolman John Forsythe is shown here in 1930. The following year, he was presented with a Hendricks Medal for his capture of Vincent Starowicz. Starowicz had shot a man during a holdup at Elk Hotel in East Syracuse and confessed to several gas station holdups during the ensuing investigation. (Courtesy of Mark Forsythe.)

This photograph of patrolman John Forsythe's children playing on his motorcycle provides a good example of the sidecars that were found on some of the police motorcycles in the 1930s. (Courtesy of Mark Forsythe.)

The 16-man Motorcycle Squad was assembled in the 100 block of West Willow Street on March 13, 1930, to receive orders and assignments from Sgt. John Costello under the watchful eye of Capt. Michael McCarthy (standing at left next to pole). It was the kickoff of a vigorous spring traffic enforcement campaign that would send more than 100 violators a day to traffic court. (Courtesy of Mark Forsythe.)

In 1934, the Motorcycle Squad lines up in front of city hall to show off new black-and-silver motorcycles. From left to right are Frank Silky, John Forsythe, Arthur Longley, George Easterly, Martin Walsh, William Gillette, Harry Green, Frederick Baty, Welcome Nuffer, and Paul Marcette. (Courtesy of Syracuse Police Archives.)

Patrolman Andrew Peltz is seen on motorcycle patrol sometime in the 1940s. Over the course of his 35 years, Peltz would command every division in the police department and rise to the rank of inspector in 1970. He was very knowledgeable on the subject of police department history and was the source people went to when such questions arose. (Courtesy of Russell Gates.)

This photograph of the Motorcycle Squad was taken in front of the Soldiers and Sailors Monument in Clinton Square sometime after May 23, 1949. On that date, motorcycle patrolmen were required to replace their traditional white summer shirt with gray shirts with highly visible traffic-insignia shoulder patches. Because of the angle of the shot, none of the patches are in view. (Courtesy of Syracuse Police Archives.)

This formation of motorcycle patrolmen attracted the attention of pedestrians and motorists alike in June 1951 as they rode south on North State Street between North Salina Street and Prospect Avenue. The General Gustavus Sniper Monument can be seen between the first two officers on the left. From left to right are unidentified, Nicholas Demperio, William Roberts, unidentified, Mercer Weiskotten, and unidentified. (Courtesy of Syracuse Police Archives.)

This photograph from the late 1950s shows members of the Motorcycle Squad lined up at Erie Boulevard West and North Clinton Street. From left are to right are patrolmen Nicholas Margiasso, five unidentified, Nicholas Demperio, unidentified, Ralph Margiasso, two unidentified, John O'Malley, Frank Montalto, two unidentified, Joseph B. Vogt, and unidentified. O'Malley was a New York state trooper before joining the police department. He later served as chief of police for the village of Minoa. (Courtesy of Syracuse Police Archives.)

Members of the Traffic Unit pose in the early 1960s. From left to right are (seated) unidentified, Robert Campagna, Nicholas Demperio, unidentified, and Jack Denero; (standing) Lt. Charles Dawson, three unidentified officers, Raymond Kramer, and Robert Smith. Robert Smith served for a time as president of the Police Benevolent Association. (Courtesy of Syracuse Police Archives.)

These motorcycle officers are leading a patriotic parade westbound on Erie Boulevard West through Clinton Square during the 1960s. Though the Soldiers and Sailors Monument has remained, much of the surrounding landscape has changed. The building in the background has been replaced by the Post Standard Newspaper Building. That block of Erie Boulevard has since been closed and replaced with an ice-skating rink and fountain where numerous festivals are held annually. (Courtesy of Syracuse Police Archives.)

Motorcycle patrolman John Hayes was awarded the Hendricks Medal in 1955 for his rescue of an 18-month-old child from a burning building. He was on patrol on February 12, 1955, when he discovered a fire in an apartment building at 713 East Fayette Street. Hayes climbed through a window and rescued the child before nearly being overcome by smoke. (Courtesy of Syracuse Police Archives.)

Lewis Felber was appointed to the police department in 1963. Motorcycle patrolman was one of his early assignments and one that he especially enjoyed. Felber is seen here patrolling the 300 block of South Salina Street in the mid-1960s. He was later assigned as an investigator in the Youth Division, and for the last 18 years of his 32-year career, he was assigned to the Criminal Investigation Division. (Courtesy of David Sackett.)

From left to right, motorcycle police officers Robert Yoder, Lewis Felber, Kenneth Yackel, Joseph Willis, Thomas Stimson, Robert Boyer, John Bozuto, and Capt. Donald Sheridan line up in the Public Safety Building courtyard. (Courtesy of Syracuse Police Archives.)

Policeman Walter Czerniel was at South Warren and East Jefferson Streets when he received some direction from the concerned citizen seated on his Harley Davidson Servi-Car in 1978. Servi-Cars were used during winter months when weather precluded the use of two-wheeled motorcycles. (Courtesy of Mark Czerniel.)

The Syracuse Police Motorcycle Squad is pictured in front of the Public Safety Building in 1978. From left to right are Lt. Peter Wright, community service officer Gabe Ramos, Sgts. William Nurk and Carl Hoyt, and police officers James Reagan, Michael Sitnik, Thomas Stimson, Edward Yaroski, Robert Kellogg, Robert Boyer, John Bozzuto, and John Boyd. (Courtesy of James Reagan.)

Chief Thomas J. Sardino inspects the Motorcycle Squad on South Townsend Street behind the Public Safety Building in the early 1970s. From left to right are police officers Thomas Stimson, William Moore, Joseph Willis, Kenneth Yackel, John Bozzuto, Robert Boyer, Otis Thompson, John Fragola, and Louis Sposato, Sgt. Peter Wright, Lt. Joseph Jaworski, Capt. Charles Dawson, and Chief Thomas Sardino. (Courtesy of Syracuse Police Archives.)

From left to right, motorcycle police officers Michael Sitnik, James Reagan, and John Morris stand by in the 100 block of West Water Street in preparation for the United Way parade on November 12, 1977. The motorcycle officers at that time were under the command of the Special Events Section. (Courtesy of James Reagan.)

After spending a number of years in Patrol and Special Events, police officer James Reagan (left) completed his career as an investigator in the Licensing Bureau. Police officer Michael Sitnik (center) joined the police department as a trainee. The program was open to youths 17 years of age and older. When they reached their 20th birthday, as Sitnik did on February 23, 1970, they were sworn in as police officers. (Courtesy of James Reagan.)

During the summer months, many Syracuse police officers work on an overtime basis, providing police coverage for city parks and swimming pools. Police officers James Reagan and Donald Shaw are shown in this 1965 photograph providing just such coverage in Thornden Park in the university section of the city. (Courtesy of James Reagan.)

It was not easy catching them, and these officers look rather pleased with themselves. From left to right, Sgt. Keith Gates and police officers John Hayes and Gary Bulinski pose next to their motorcycles with US Navy Blue Angels jets behind them. The photograph was taken at the Syracuse Hancock International Airport. The airport was known for many years as Hancock Field, and it is the home of the 174th Fighter Wing of the New York Air National Guard, affectionately known as the "Boys from Syracuse." (Courtesy of Syracuse Police Archives.)

The police department put this automobile on the streets of Syracuse in 1906. It was manufactured in Syracuse by the Franklin Automobile Company, which was located on South Geddes Street where Fowler High School now stands. Showing off the new car in September 1906 are, from left to right, Deputy Chief William O'Brien, Det. James Sheppard, a chauffeur identified only as Ted, and Chief Martin Caden while patrolmen Franklin Sheriff and William Austin look on. (Courtesy of Syracuse Police Archives.)

This car was assigned to the Accident Investigation Division of the police department in the 1940s. Like all accident division cars, it was painted yellow so that it could be immediately recognizable. The cars could be quickly converted for ambulance duty by changing the rear seats into beds. The cars were also equipped with first-aid equipment. (Courtesy of Syracuse Police Archives.)

This photograph was taken early in 1957. By the end of the year, the tote board on top of the car would list 12 traffic fatalities for the year, two fewer than the year before. Though still high, it was proof that aggressive traffic enforcement was making a difference. Between 1928 and December 1957, a total of 631 people had been killed in automobile mishaps, with 37 occurring in 1929 alone. (Courtesy of Syracuse Police Archives.)

Patrolman James Davis is seen in a black-and-white patrol car in the late 1960s. A few years later, the department changed back to white patrol cars. (Courtesy of James Davis.)

In 1943, the Syracuse Police Department experimented with white patrol cars based on a recommendation of the Volmer Plan. The decision was very unpopular with the rank and file officers, as was the plan itself. The color scheme was abandoned until years later when cost factors prompted the return of white cars. This 1975 Plymouth Fury is an example. (Courtesy of Syracuse Police Archives.)

Within several years, other local agencies were shifting to the use of white patrol cars as well, including the Onondaga County Sheriff's Office. To make city police cars more easily distinguishable from other agencies, Chief Thomas Sardino ordered a change to a blue similar to that used by the New York Police Department. This 1985 Plymouth above was the first variation. It was later refined in the 1990s, as can be seen with this Chevrolet Impala below. (Both, courtesy of Syracuse Police Archives.)

By the late 1990s, the cost of custom paint was once again a factor in the decision to return to white patrol cars. Additionally, the larger Impala body style was being discontinued, so the Ford Crown Victoria took its place in the Syracuse police fleet. (Courtesy of Syracuse Police Archives.)

Interestingly, with the return to the traditional black-and-white patrol cars came new technologies. Current patrol cars are equipped with computer terminals on which reports are written, complaints are received, and traffic tickets are filled out and printed. GPS can pinpoint the location and route of travel of the vehicle at any time. (Courtesy of Syracuse Police Archives.)

In 1927, chief of police Martin Cadin began lobbying for an airplane for the police department to use in hunting criminals. He proposed that when the plane was not being used for police purposes, it could be utilized for conducting municipal surveys. By January 1928, the city had agreed to purchase the aircraft. The estimated cost for the plane was $2,000, and the plan called for it to be hangered at the municipal airport in Amboy. The plane was in fact purchased, but little can be found regarding its use after that. (Courtesy of Edward Taglialatela.)

The Syracuse Police Department and the Onondaga County Sheriff's Office began a program on June 24, 1975, called Operation AIR STOP. With three Army surplus helicopters and a federal grant of $178,000 to prepare the ships and train pilots, they took to the air. Each department was assigned one helicopter, and a third served as a backup. They were based at Timbello's Helicopters on Bridge Street in East Syracuse. Pictured above at Timbello's on June 24, 1975, are, from left to right, two unidentified men in civilian attire, Sgt. Michael Boylan, and police officers Gary Peak and Roger Baker. The photograph below shows pilot Roger Baker (seated) and observer Ron Buczakowski (standing on the other side of the ship) in 1977. (Above, courtesy of Syracuse Police Archives; below, courtesy of Roger Baker.)

For a brief time, the police department used this boat for its short-lived Marine Unit. The barge canal and the south end of Onondaga Lake cut into the city's north side. The boat promised to be an important safety and enforcement tool with the promise of inner-harbor development. Under New York State law, because Onondaga Lake stretched into the city, the police department had jurisdiction anywhere on the body of water and on all of its tributaries. Officers were assigned to man the vessel in pairs on an overtime basis. Inspector James Boynton is facing the camera in the above photograph. The sergeant piloting the boat is unidentified. Police officer John Hayes (left) and Sgt. Geoffrey Ciereck (right) are seen below. (Both, courtesy of Syracuse Police Archives.)

Four

People, Places, and Events

Abraham Prettie spent much of his police career as a roundsman, which is a supervisory rank used in the early years of policing. It was the equivalent of the current rank of sergeant. Prettie also held the rank of acting captain briefly in 1883, and at the time of his retirement in 1886, he held the position of inspector of uniforms. (Courtesy of Syracuse Police Archives.)

Patrolman Timothy Driscoll was appointed to the police department December 1, 1899. He served until the time of his death at age 55 on December 2, 1911. He was followed in service with the Syracuse Police Department by his grandson Thomas Driscoll and his great-grandson James Driscoll. (Courtesy of James Driscoll.)

Patrolman Charles Goetel was appointed to the police department on October 15, 1885, and he served until his death on March 26, 1869. This photograph of him depicts the uniform of that era. His grayish-brown derby indicates that this picture was probably taken sometime during the summer months, as winter headgear was typically dark in color. (Courtesy of Russell Gates.)

Patrolman Daniel Lee was appointed to the police department on June 1, 1880. He was assigned to the "Dog Watch" (4:00 a.m.–1:00 p.m.) until he was eventually appointed to the rank of detective to fill a vacancy following the death of Det. Charles Doolittle. Among some of the more noteworthy of Lee's cases was his apprehension of three members of the notorious Marwin Gang of pickpockets. (Courtesy of John Hierholzer.)

Policeman Paul Hart served as a member of the police department from October 1, 1901, to August 29, 1911, when he died of a heart attack. He was considered a model policeman and one of the most popular men on the force. A member of the Traffic Squad, few would pass his post at East Genesee and South Warren Streets without making a point of addressing him. (Courtesy of Richard Goldacker.)

On May 3, 1894, August Decker was appointed to the police department as a patrolman. He served in that capacity until February 1901 when the rank of police sergeant was created and he was promoted. Sergeant Decker continued his service energetically for another 27 years before he reached the mandatory retirement age of 65 and was forced to retire in May 1928, bringing to an end his 34-year police career. (Courtesy of Thomas Murfitt.)

Sgt. Frank Lesicki was appointed to the police department in 1927. During his many years with the department, Sergeant Lesicki trained hundreds of police officers in the use of firearms. He was also captain of the Syracuse Police Pistol Team, and by the time of his retirement, he had earned 102 trophies and numerous firearms medals. As a Marine, he served on the president's yacht and as part of the Honor Guards for Secretary of the Navy Denby and Pres. Calvin Coolidge. (Courtesy of Russell Gates.)

Patrolman Andrew Wolfrom was seriously injured on August 22, 1936, when he aided patrolman William Brody, who was being attacked by a large group of violent strikers during the Remington Rand labor strike on Gifford Street. Wolfrom sustained a fractured skull, broken ribs, and kidney damage. Wolfrom was finally able to return to work October 1, 1936. After he returned, however, his condition continued to decline, and he died February 1, 1937. (Courtesy of the family of Andrew Wolfrom.)

Lt. William Adams (left) and Inspector Pasquale Bennett (right) are pictured on December 27, 1945. Adams was appointed to the police department on April 24, 1911. For 11 years, he commanded the municipal parks details, which included the mounted patrols. He was then assigned to the Municipal Airport, and for his final year, Adams commanded the night foot patrols. Bennett began his career on February 12, 1906, when he was appointed Italian interpreter. On December 30, 1907, he was appointed detective without ever having performed patrol duty. Pasquale Bennett served on the department for 40 years. (Courtesy of Syracuse Police Archives.)

In November 1926, the Syracuse Police Department went to a precinct system. Newly appointed Capt. Pasquale Bennett (left) was placed in command of Precinct 2, the Burnet Park station. The patrolman on the right is unidentified. (Courtesy of Syracuse Police Archives.)

Patrolman John Cusick was appointed to the police department in 1918. He was struck down by a car while he was assigned to school traffic duty at the intersection of South Avenue and Jackson Street. He eventually returned to duty and worked for a time as a turnkey before retiring on October 22, 1943. (Courtesy of Katherine Foley.)

John Holihan spent more than 28 years on the Syracuse Police Department. He rose through the ranks. For a period, he commanded the Traffic Unit, and in 1964, Chief William H.T. Smith promoted him to the rank of first deputy chief. Following his retirement from the department, Holihan became chief of the Alexandria Police Department in Virginia. (Courtesy of Syracuse Police Archives.)

Sgt. David Brown was appointed to the police department on May 18, 1879. He worked as a popular and dependable patrolman until July 13, 1895, when he was promoted to the rank of sergeant, replacing the recently deceased Sgt. William Rapp. Sergeant Brown commanded the Dog Watch until his resignation on January 6, 1902, following a reorganization that reassigned him to command the 12:00 p.m.–8:00 p.m. shift. (Courtesy of John Hierholzer.)

Willie Gilbert was appointed to the police department in 1951, becoming Syracuse's first African American police officer. During his service with the police department, Gilbert worked a number of assignments, including foot patrol, internal affairs, and criminal investigations. He retired from the department in 1987. (Courtesy of Christopher Lamontagne.)

Shown is the rookie class of January 16, 1957. Pictured from left to right are police chief Harold F. Kelly, Peter J. Wright, Charles Kriese, Vince Quatrone, John Donahue, James G. Reagan, Robert McCabe, James McNamara, Carmen Surace, "Butch" Hennessey, John Maas, Arthur Peck, Alfred Reagan, Edward Lipena, David Utt, Samuel Longo, Robert Alexander, and Knobby Sheridan. (Courtesy of James Reagan.)

Police officer Paul Hudson is pictured in the Public Safety Building courtyard during the early 1970s. He was one of the earliest members of the Emergency Service Unit, which is no longer operational. Members were required to be emergency medical technicians in addition to their police duties. Hudson left the unit and became one of the first two K-9 officers for the police department. (Courtesy of Cynthia Gates.)

Police officers (left, in front of and behind first flag) and firemen (right) are formed at city hall for the 1945 medals ceremony. Police officers are, from left to right, (first row) Samuel Nappi and John Bienkowski; (second row) Clarence Snow, George Webster, and Charles Dawson; (third row) Harold Shea, Michael Joyce, Emil Kempf, Solvatore Solvato, and William Silky; (fourth row) Clifford Ours and George Easterly; (fifth row) William Metzger, John Forsythe, William Seidenfus, Harold Garn, and Francis Garn. Nappi received the Hendricks Medal, while Bienkowski was presented with the Herald Medal. (Courtesy of Syracuse Police Archives.)

Police officers and sergeants are gathered in the Drill Room of the Willow Street station for daily roll call and to be addressed by the chief before taking to the streets for the 12:00 p.m.–4:00 a.m. shift in 1949. The Drill Room was usually the center of activity at police headquarters. (Courtesy of Syracuse Police Archives.)

On June 23, 1930, Marguerite Hannon, wife of patrolman James Hannon, accepted the Herald Medal awarded posthumously to her husband. Patrolman Hannon had been shot during a burglary in progress and died during later surgery. Patrolman George Easterly (right) was awarded the Hendricks Medal for his pursuit and apprehension of a robbery suspect who had beaten a downtown pawnbroker. (Courtesy of Syracuse Police Archives.)

In this undated photograph, Marguerite Hannon is joined by Mayor Thomas Young following a medals ceremony. She is holding the uniform hat worn by her husband, James, on the fateful night in 1929 when he interrupted a burglary in progress at Walker's drugstore on South Crouse Avenue. (Courtesy of Syracuse Police Archives.)

Police officer Victor McNett is prepared for pre-parade inspection with his neatly trimmed, newly acquired mustache. This photograph was taken on August 14, 1948, before Syracuse's centennial parade. Victor would attain the rank of lieutenant and command the crime lab before his retirement. (Courtesy of Victor McNett.)

Syracuse has a long tradition of having the police department lead its parades. The city's centennial parade, held on August 14, 1948, featured Syracuse's own Keystone Cops. Shown from left to right, police officers Victor McNett, George Kappesser, Bernard Weber, and Herbert Lavere mount up in preparation for the festivities of the day. (Courtesy of Victor McNett.)

The Syracuse Police Pistol Team, undefeated during the 1949–1950 Syracuse Pistol League season, presents their trophy to Chief John Kinney (third from right). The team consisted of, from left to right, patrolmen Chester Piatkowski and Robert Chappel, Sgt. Frank Lesicki, Det. Bernard Nelson, and patrolmen James Considine and Robert Vuillemot. All were veterans of World War II, except the sergeant who was a veteran of World War I. (Courtesy of Syracuse Police Archives.)

The police department staged Police Night on March 12, 1969, at the Onondaga County War Memorial. It was an event held to acquaint the community with the police department and introduce 45 newly graduated law enforcement recruits, who were sworn in during the affair. A number of demonstrations were also performed, including this marksmanship demonstration by policeman Joseph Morabito, Sgt. Walter Sloan, and policeman Chester Piatkowski, seen above from left to right. (Courtesy of Syracuse Police Archives.)

Meter maid Elaine English is seen here applying a bumper sticker to a patrol car to launch a safe driving campaign in 1962 as Chief Harold Kelley (center) and an unidentified gentleman look on. They are on West Genesee Street in front of police headquarters. Visible in the background is the old US Post Office, which currently houses the offices of Pyramid Construction. (Courtesy of Syracuse Police Archives.)

Samuel Nappi (left) and Charles Dawson (right) clown around on the occasion of their promotions to the rank of sergeant. Both men were members of the Blue Ribbon Squad. All of the squad members were sworn in together in 1942. It was the first recruit class that required everyone to have a high school diploma. They remained a close-knit group throughout their careers, celebrating anniversary dates regularly. Every one of them attained a gold badge rank. (Courtesy of Syracuse Police Archives.)

On March 5, 1953, area police were invited to check out the Bent Rods Hot Rod Club at 465 Pulaski Street. Pictured are, from left to right, Frank Allen, club vice president; patrolman Harold Gronau and Chief Floyd Harrison, of the Liverpool Police Department; Chief Basil Valetta, of the Solvay Police Department; Edward Karpinski, club president; Lt. Samuel Nappi, of the Syracuse Police Department; and Vincent Cook, club secretary-treasurer. (Courtesy of the family of Samuel Nappi.)

Television/movie star Nicholas Georgiadi (seated) shares a few things he learned in his role as Rico Rossi in the television series "The Untouchables" with Lt. Paul McLaughlin (left) and his brother George Georgiadi (right), who retired as a lieutenant. The three men in the middle are unidentified. (Courtesy of Syracuse Police Archives.)

On September 6, 1954, Sgt. Frank Lesicki exhibits firearms and other equipment at a police department display during a three-day convention held by the Greater Syracuse Safety Council at the Hotel Syracuse. (Both, courtesy of Syracuse Police Archives.)

The police department in coordination with the Police Benevolent Association sponsored a Syracuse Police Scholarship Foundation benefit baseball game at MacArthur Stadium on August 25, 1965. Among the night's events were several rank promotions: Richard Schill to captain, Edward Corbett and Bernard Weber to lieutenant, and Thomas Driscoll, Donald Shea, Joseph Molica, and Manuel Leone to sergeant. Capt. John Litcher and Chief William H.T. Smith made the presentations. (Courtesy of Syracuse Police Archives.)

In addition to his police department duties, Police Benevolent Association (PBA) president Robert Powers managed this PBA-sponsored Southside Little League team. (Courtesy of Syracuse Police Archives.)

Members of the Syracuse Police Benevolent Association basketball team are pictured on January 9, 1949. From left to right are (first row) Richard Currier, William Busch, and Charles Kraft; (second row) Andrew Linehan (coach), George Turo, Herman Schultz, William Franey, John Dixon, Samuel Nappi, and Casmir Chorazy (manager); (third row) Joseph Franey, Dolly Henry, Robert Alexander, John Gossin, Donald Green, and Thomas Hurley. (Courtesy of the *Post Standard*.)

The Police Benevolent Association sponsored this touch football team in the 1970s. Pictured from left to right are (first row) Jerry Dain, Frank Palotta, Brian Murphy, Steven Thompson, Joseph Rappazzo, John Corbett, William Rybak, Timothy Mumford, and Tony Mangel; (second row) John Putnam, Robert Duchessi, Michael Baker, Michael Sitnick, Bruce Nill, Louie Brunelle, John Marcon, William Kocher, Brian McGraw, and Richard Haumann. (Courtesy of Syracuse Police Archives.)

Ernie Davis played football for Syracuse University when he won the Heisman Trophy in 1961, becoming the first African American to do so. Following his death in 1963, the trophy was donated to the university by his mother. On March 31, 1976, it was stolen from a display case at Manley Field House. The trophy was later turned in to the *Post Standard* on April 14, 1976. The statue was turned over to police, who returned it to the university. Sgt. Richard Walsh (left) and investigator Charles Venton (right) are shown with the Heisman. (Courtesy of Daniel Walsh.)

Police officer Robert Murray (left) and Lt. Dennis O'Donnell (right) are courtside at the Carrier Dome on February 14, 1981. The Syracuse University Orangemen played the University of Connecticut Huskies, setting an NCAA attendance record with 26,257 spectators. Murray retired from the department once but returned and worked as a detective in the Criminal Investigation Division for a number of years before retiring a final time. (Courtesy of Robert Murray.)

Every year, the Syracuse Life Insurance companies present life-saving awards to deserving Syracuse police officers. On October 19, 1978, an unidentified insurance representative presented three such awards to, from left to right, police officer John Brennan, Sgt. Edward Uhlig, and police officer Gerald Sabloski. They had discovered a fire inside a building on Baker Avenue, and working in concert, they removed three people who had been sleeping in the building. (Courtesy of Edward Uhlig.)

During the 1970s, the department sponsored a very active Explorer Scout group. Some of the Scouts are seen here during a work detail at the police heliport. From left to right are police officer John Putnam, William Galvin (currently a sergeant assigned to the airport), police officer Ronald Buzakowski, unidentified, Keith Gates (retired as a sergeant), Vincent Zoll, Cynthia Gates (currently a public safety dispatcher II with Onondaga County 911), and Frank Rudy (retired as a police officer). (Courtesy of Cynthia Gates.)

Patrolman Donald Derby retired in 1991. He is seen pinning the badge that he wore for nearly 21 years on his son Thomas Derby at a Police Academy graduation ceremony on August 24, 1991. For many, service with the Syracuse Police Department has become a family tradition. (Courtesy of Syracuse Police Archives.)

Det. Daniel Walsh (left) and his father, Capt. Richard Walsh (right), are in Forman Park. Detective Walsh is wearing the department's ceremonial bagpiper uniform. This photograph was taken on Law Enforcement Day 2011 at the corner of Forman Avenue and East Genesee Street where the Syracuse Police Department's Law Enforcement Monument/Memorial is located. Portions of the monuments are visible in the background. (Courtesy of Daniel Walsh.)

This photograph was taken before the Syracuse St. Patrick's Day Parade in 1985, the first year Syracuse police officers marched in the parade. Only 10 members represented the Syracuse Police Department. They are, from left to right, Barry Murphy, Peter Tynan, Peter O'Brien, James Boynton, William Finnie, Richard Walsh, Walter Sloan, and Edward McLaughlin. James Galvin and Robert Murray arrived later and did not appear in the photograph. (Courtesy of Daniel Walsh.)

On March 12, 2011, Capt. Richard Walsh served as the grand marshal of the St. Patrick's Day parade. That day, Captain Walsh retired as the commanding officer of the Criminal Investigation Division after more than 40 years of service. Captain Walsh can be seen in this photograph in the center, wearing the grand marshal's sash as he leads the department down South Salina Street. (Courtesy of Daniel Walsh.)

Five

Investigations Bureau

Chief Det. James Sheppard was born in Dorsetshire, England, on May 12, 1848. He was appointed to the police force as a patrolman on October 23, 1873. Shepard was promoted to detective on November 4, 1881, and on June 1, 1893, he received the appointment as aide to the chief and chief detective. (Courtesy of Syracuse Police Archives.)

Charles E. Doolittle was promoted to detective in 1893 following James Harvey's murder. At the time, he was one of only three officers ever presented a medal for meritorious service. He received it for the capture of a jewelry store burglar in 1879. Doolittle was better remembered for his 1884 capture of Clarence Tear. Tear had escaped Auburn Prison, committed a series of burglaries, and exchanged gunfire with Doolittle during his capture. (Courtesy of John Hierholzer.)

In April 1915, as a result of a change of venue, the *William Barnes v. Theodore Roosevelt* libel trial was moved from Albany to a Syracuse courtroom. Former president Roosevelt (right), accompanied by his personal secretary John McGrath, walks up East Jefferson Street to the Onondaga County courthouse under the watchful eye of Det. Pasquale Bennett (center). (Courtesy of Syracuse Police Archives.)

Acting detectives John Forsythe (left) and Francis Ryan (second from left) look on as a marijuana dealer (second from right) shows State Health Department narcotics inspector Ralph Weisman (right) the article that inspired him to grow and sell marijuana to area swing and jazz musicians. At the time of his arrest at Cedar and Almond Streets on September 2, 1938, the man was selling two marijuana cigarettes for 25¢. (Courtesy of Syracuse Police Archives.)

This photograph was taken the following day when the dealer accompanied the officers to his Liverpool home to show them what remained of his operation. Detectives Forsythe (left) and Ryan (right) examine a quantity of marijuana that the young man had stored in a cigar box. (Courtesy of Syracuse Police Archives.)

The suspect in this case had heard talk on the street that the police suspected him of trafficking in marijuana. Shortly before his arrest, he had burned what was left of his crop and turned over the soil. As a result, there was little left when Det. John Forsythe inspected the area where days before the marijuana had grown. (Courtesy of Syracuse Police Archives.)

Acting detective John Forsythe (left) arrested this South Salina Street man for public intoxication on March 11, 1938, during an investigation into how he received a wound to his hand. The man claimed he was shot during a robbery attempt, but he later admitted that he was injured during a domestic dispute. (Courtesy of Syracuse Police Archives.)

A confessed murder suspect is led from the district attorney's office in the Onondaga County Courthouse following his confession on February 3, 1958. From left to right are district attorney Charles McNett, Det. Robert Klein, Chief Harold Kelley, unidentified suspect, and Det. Paul Marcette. (Courtesy of Syracuse Police Archives.)

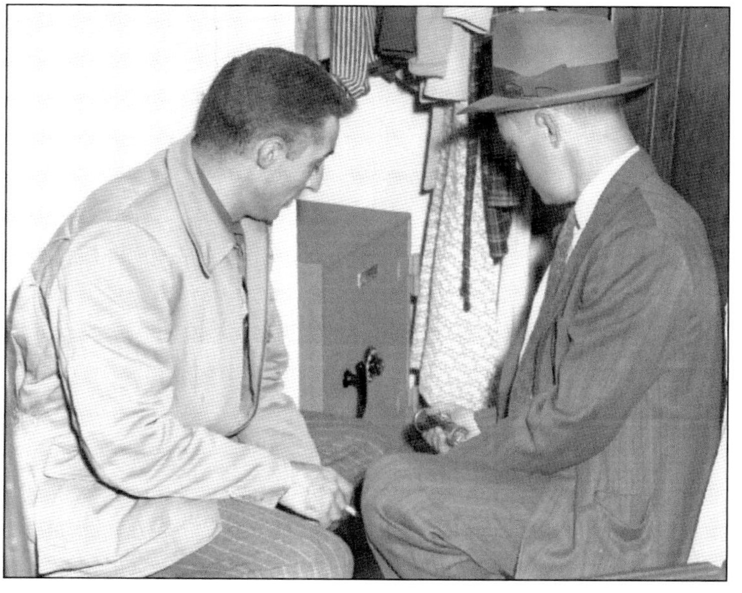

Acting detective Florin Marsallo (left) and Sgt. William McCarthy (right) examine the safe that was to have been the target of a burglary team on Hickok Avenue. Officers set up surveillance to capture them in the act. When the officers tried make the arrest, there was an exchange of gunfire, leaving two suspects wounded and one dead. (Courtesy of the family of Samuel Nappi.)

Sgt. Samuel Nappi (left) explains to Capt. William Metzger (right) how he pursued one of the suspects through several backyards after two of them fled the residence, firing gunshots. Nappi shot and wounded the suspect before he finally was able to capture him. (Courtesy of the family of Samuel Nappi.)

Capt. William Metzger (left) returned fire when one suspect exited the house, firing at police. The captain's shotgun blast struck and killed the suspect. He and Nappi (right) examine where Metzger's first shot struck the house. (Courtesy of the family of Samuel Nappi.)

Sgt. William McCarthy tends to burglar Joseph DiPasquale, who was wounded in the gunfight with police. (Courtesy of the family of Samuel Nappi.)

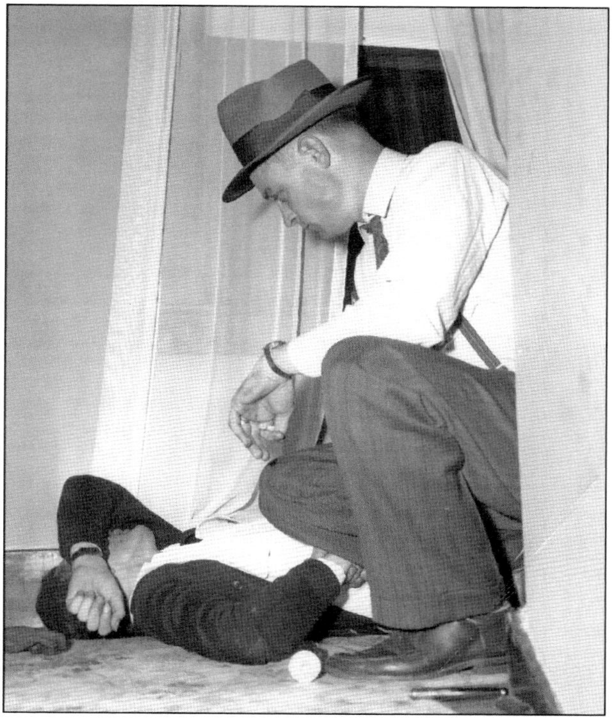

Sgt. William McCarthy and Capt. William Metzger look on as an unidentified detective examines the revolver next to the body the burglar killed in the exchange of gunfire. This case was dramatized on the nationally broadcast CBS program *Gang Busters* in 1951. (Courtesy of the family of Samuel Nappi.)

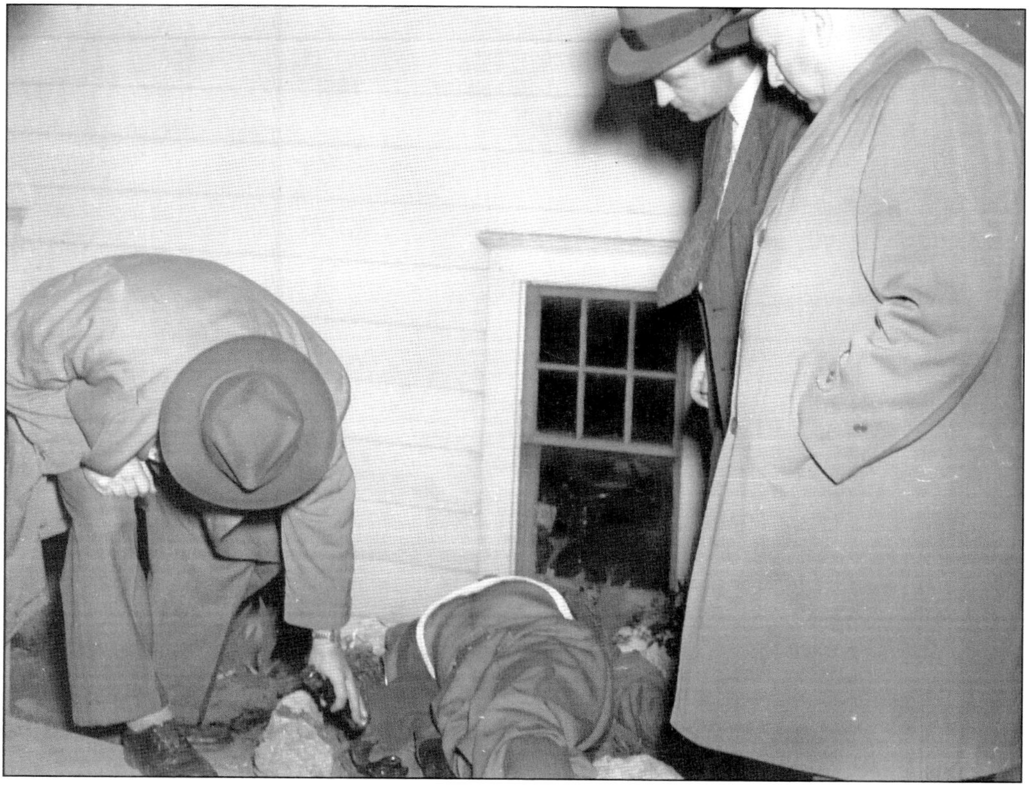

Investigator Henry Chanley is pictured on January 31, 1967, transporting a bank robber to the Public Safety Building following a robbery at the Marine Midland Trust Company at 711 Erie Boulevard East. On January 23, 1967, the suspect entered the bank armed with a handgun and demanded money from a teller. Once he had the money, he ran out of the bank and down Foreman Avenue. He was later apprehended in New York City. (Courtesy of Syracuse Police Archives.)

Patrolman Arthur Dudden (left) stands by as investigator Henry Chanley walks a prisoner to the wagon following a gambling raid. In the background between the suspect and Chanley is investigator Theodore Kaskey. Behind Chanley in black is investigator Ronald Arroway. The photograph was taken approximately 1964 on North Salina Street. The Assumption Church steeple is seen in the background. (Courtesy of Syracuse Police Archives.)

Investigator Donald Shea (left) is shown interviewing a burglary suspect along with an unidentified New York state trooper (center). Shea also served as chauffeur and bodyguard for Mayor William Walsh until August 1965. When Chief Smith restructured the department, Shea was transferred to the Organized Crime Division and promoted to the rank of sergeant. (Courtesy of Donald Shea.)

Investigators John Burke Jr. and Henry Chanley take aim at June 12, 1965, as a target date for the 30th annual Policemen's Ball. The affair was held at the war memorial, and the Glenn Miller Band was the entertainment. (Courtesy of Syracuse Police Archives.)

On February 6, 1963, investigator Henry Chanley made the mistake of parking his personal vehicle on West Genesee Street outside the police station, which can be seen in the background on the left side of the photograph. Chanley was actually using his car for work. Investigators had the option of using their personal vehicles and fueling them with city gas. Officers pictured are Raymond Cramer (left), Ronald Arroway (in the foreground), and Sgt. Michael Krisak (right). The motorcycle officer on top of the car is unidentified. (Courtesy of Henry Chanley.)

Investigator Edward Uhlig displays the results of a drug investigation in the early 1970s when marijuana plants, such as these, constituted much more serious offense than they have in recent years. (Courtesy of Edward Uhlig.)

On March 16, 1982, a body was found in an unused loading dock on State Fair Boulevard after the snow that filled it thawed. It was subsequently determined that the victim had died of natural causes. Investigating are, from left to right, Lt. Richard Walsh, Capt. Walter Sloan, Deputy Chief Joseph Jewell, investigators George Raugh and Richard Goldacker, and police officer William Cinciolla. (Courtesy of Syracuse Police Archives.)

Members of the Burglary Squad take an individual into custody in the late 1980s. They are, from left to right, investigator Dean Panarites, Sgt. John Brennan, Sgt. James Driscoll, and police officer Raymond Barringer. (Courtesy of Capt. John Brennan.)

The Selective Enforcement Unit (Burglary Squad) is gathered to celebrate the holidays. They are, from left to right, (first row) Daniel Malay, James Quatrone, and John Mulherin; (second row) Patrick Lynch, Michael Rathbun, Timothy Flynn, Nick Vassinelli, Michael Walsh, Joseph Smola, Robert Teater, Pierre Patnode, Patrick Conley, and Gary Coe. (Courtesy of Patrick Lynch.)

The members of the Burglary Squad take time out from their night assignment in the early 2000s for this picture. From left to right are investigators Edward MacBlane, John Savage, Paul Kluge, Gordon Quonce, James Quatrone, and Robert Teater; Sgt. Donald Hilton; investigators Thomas Derby, Todd Hood, Joseph Smola, Steven Stonecypher, Mark Abraham, Nicholas Vassinelli, and Gary Coe. (Courtesy of Thomas Derby.)

Six

Uniform Bureau

In the mid-1930s, these officers gathered around the front desk make up the Traffic Division of the Syracuse Police Department. They were responsible for the enforcement of traffic laws in general, but they placed a high priority on the enforcement of speed violations. Additionally, they were responsible for accident investigations. From left to right are patrolmen Kenneth MacDonald, James McCormick, Hyacinth Luebberman, Edward Bachman, and Martin Costello. (Courtesy of Syracuse Police Archives.)

The 1928 Motorcycle Squad was made up of the police officers pictured above. From left to right are patrolmen Sylvester Coogan, George Easterly, Patrick Hanlon, Frank C. Flath, Ralph Margiasso, John L. Barry, and John Costello. (Courtesy of Daniel Walsh.)

Paul Marcette (right), pictured here speaking with an unidentified motorcycle patrolman, spent many years of his career on motorcycles. In later years, he became a very capable detective. In that position, Marcette was responsible for investigating a number of narcotics cases. At the time of this photograph, officers were required to wear white shirts during the summer. There was no standard necktie, as can be seen by the plaid tie that Marcette is wearing. (Courtesy of Russell Gates.)

Patrolman Paul Marcette (far left) can be seen once again in this photograph from the same era. He and an unidentified officer are ensuring the safe delivery of a wagon load of beer to Lou's Tavern at 141 James Street. (Courtesy of Syracuse Police Archives.)

The front desk at police headquarters was the nerve center of the department. Personnel staffing it were expected to address walk-in issues, review officer's paperwork, provide information to the public and police personnel, and have knowledge of current police activities. It remains so today. Pictured are, from left to right, Lt. Harry Harrington, Sgt. Frank Lesicki, and patrolman William Silky on desk duty at the old Willow Street police station in July 1949. (Courtesy of Syracuse Police Archives.)

Albany kidnappers Harold "Red" Crowley, John J. Oley, and Percy "Angel Face" Geary were being held in Jamesville (Onondaga County) Penitentiary awaiting transportation to the federal penitentiary at Alcatraz when Geary sawed his way out of his cell. He held five guards and a matron at gunpoint, released Crowley and Oley, and they made their escape. Hundreds of city, county, state, and federal law enforcement officers participated in the ensuing manhunt, known as the "Great Chase." Crowley and Oley are seen here following their dramatic recapture in a Burnet Avenue rooming house on November 17, 1937. From left to right are patrolman Harold Kelley, patrolman James Heffer, Crowley, patrolman Robert Holland, Oley, unidentified, and Lt. John Ebinger. Percy Geary was captured two days later when a parking lot attendant who let him stay in his shelter at Erie Boulevard East and Pearl Street recognized Geary and alerted police. During the search and captures, not a shot was fired, but New York State police sergeant Joseph Fitzpatrick was killed in a patrol car crash after 48 hours on roadblock duty. (Courtesy of Russell Gates.)

To extricate the injured operator of this vehicle, Sgt. Samuel Nappi uses a pry bar to force open the door of a vehicle that had collided with a tractor-trailer at Butternut and First North Streets on August 1, 1951. (Courtesy of the family of Samuel Nappi.)

These unidentified officers were working out of the Burnet Park precinct in the late 1920s or early 1930s. The precinct served the Skunk City and Tipperary Hill sections of the city, as well as Burnet Park and the zoo. (Courtesy of Syracuse Police Archives.)

In June 1924, patrolman Andrew A. Nelipowitz (left) became the second recipient of the Hendricks Medal for actions earlier that year. While at the scene of a building fire, patrolman Nelipowitz observed a woman trapped on the second floor of the burning structure. He persuaded her to jump from her position into his arms below. Though injured as a result of the feat, patrolman Andrew Nelipowitz saved the life of the woman. (Courtesy of the family of Andrew Nelipowitz.)

On February 19, 1941, fire broke out in the Whitlock Building at 476–480 South Salina Street. The fire department poured water onto the Whitlock and surrounding buildings for three days in freezing temperatures, encasing the block in ice. The 400 block of South Salina Street, the main thoroughfare through the city, remained closed while this unidentified Syracuse officer guarded the fire scene. (Courtesy of Russell Gates.)

This parked car did not stay that way after the nurse who owned it forgot to set the handbrake when she left it behind Syracuse Memorial Hospital on July 8, 1948. Patrolmen Paul Marcetti (left) and John Shostack (right) investigate after the car rolled across the driveway and 130 feet over an embankment before striking the tree. (Courtesy of Syracuse Police Archives.)

Patrolman William Sushereba (right) was showing this unidentified young officer some of the finer points of directing traffic in the 200 block of James Street during the 1940s. Sushereba spent much of his time with the police department in the Traffic Division. He was promoted to the rank of lieutenant before he retired, and he was followed into the police department by his son William. (Courtesy of Syracuse Police Archives.)

This photograph of Sgt. Frank Lesicki (right) meeting with an unidentified officer appears to have been taken in early July 1950. Effective July 2, 1950, all uniform officers were ordered to wear gray shirts in the summer instead of the traditional white shirt. Local suppliers, however, could not immediately meet the demand, so for a brief period, both shirts were authorized. (Courtesy of Russell Gates.)

Patrolman Donald Shea checks the door of a business at Almond and East Fayette Streets at 3:00 a.m. while patrolman John P. Leahey mans car 62 on September 16, 1949. While Leahey covered his normal 8:00 p.m.–4:00 a.m. shift, Shea was newly appointed, so he attended police school from 2:00 p.m.–4:00 p.m., and then he worked patrol from 10:00 p.m.–4:00 a.m. (Courtesy of Donald Shea.)

There was a time when the Syracuse Police Department worked very closely with railroad police. A number of city officers left the department to work for the railroad. The New York Central Railroad police in particular were trained in the Syracuse academy. The once bustling freight yard along Erie Boulevard West is quiet now. On June 11, 1952, a steer belonging to the Fairway Packing Company escaped while it was being loaded onto a freight train. It rampaged through the 600 block of Erie Boulevard West, eluding nine police officers for an hour and a half before Sgt. Samuel Nappi was forced to shoot it. (Both, courtesy of Syracuse Police Archives.)

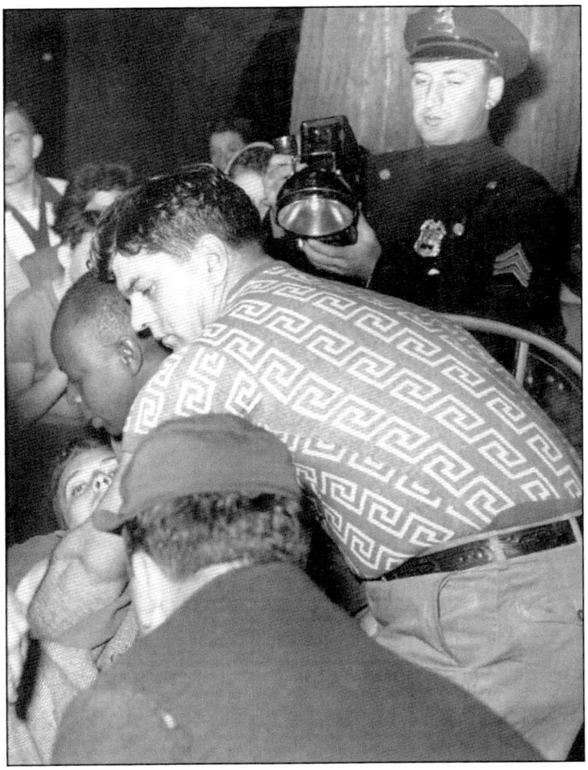

The Traffic Squad of the 1940s was charged with reducing the number of traffic mishaps through the enforcement of speed and other vehicle and traffic laws. Many of the police officers who were assigned to the squad went on to achieve high ranks. Members of the 1940s Traffic Squad pictured are, from left to right, (first row) John Holihan, Samuel Nappi, William Delaney, Howard Shea, and Francis Biel; (second row) Francis Santiff, Emil Kocher, William Franey, William Sushereba, and Donald Sheridan. (Courtesy of Syracuse Police Archives.)

A Morristown, New Jersey, man crashed his car at South McBride and East Adams Streets on April 8, 1951. Police and fire rescuers had to cut away parts of the vehicle to extricate him. Sgt. Samuel Nappi can be seen at the top of this picture as he holds a light for those rescuers. (Courtesy of the family of Samuel Nappi.)

The safety of children has always been a year-round concern for the police department. Halloween, however, can present its own unique safety issues for children. That was the case on October 31, 1945, when patrolman Samuel Nappi accompanied a group of children on their trick-or-treat mission at Smith and Jackson Streets. It remains a priority today. (Courtesy of the family of Samuel Nappi.)

Sgt. Samuel Nappi examines the damages to both vehicles involved in this traffic crash on March 29, 1948. The automobile was driven under the back of the truck, and six people were injured in the crash, which occurred in the 800 block of Erie Boulevard East. (Courtesy of the family of Samuel Nappi.)

No record has been found that there was any official recognition for this rescue, but when fire broke out in Mangel's store on March 9, 1950, patrolman Paul Marcette was quick to act. The fire started in the front window display area. It caused considerable damage to the first and second floors, but Marcette minimized the loss by removing what merchandise and fixtures he could. (Courtesy of Syracuse Police Archives.)

There clearly was a parking or perhaps a failed-to-yield-the-right-of-way violation when police officer James Driscoll and his unidentified partner investigate this crash that involved an automobile driven into a house during the 1940s. (Courtesy of James Driscoll.)

Patrolman James Driscoll was part of a law enforcement family tradition. His grandfather Timothy Driscoll had preceded him in service with the Syracuse Police Department, and his son James followed him. He retired from the police department as a detective sergeant. (Courtesy of James Driscoll.)

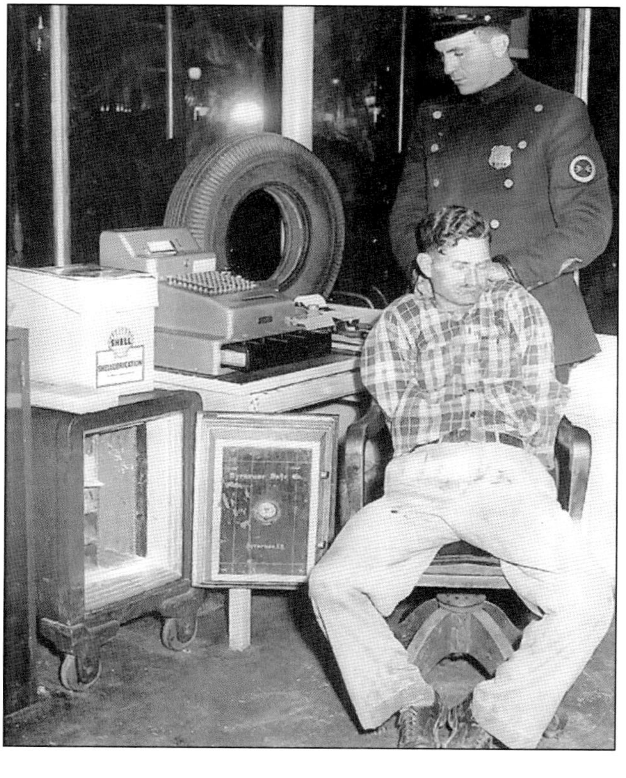

Patrolman James Driscoll was dispatched to a burglary at a gas station at 666 West Genesee Street on April 24, 1951. When he arrived, he spotted this suspect squatting in front of the safe, but he had disappeared by the time the officer got inside. Driscoll eventually found the burglar dangling from the underside of a truck in the grease pit. The arrest was one of two for which Driscoll was awarded the Arthur Jenkins Award. (Courtesy of James Driscoll.)

In August 1967, police personnel lead a suspect from his West Belden Avenue home in handcuffs after he threatened his family and police with a rifle. Police investigator Joseph T. Heick was able to disarm the suspect. He was taken into custody by (from left to right) Sgt. James Driscoll, investigator John Mahar, policeman Thomas Tangredi, and Sgt. Henry Boyle. (Both, courtesy of James Driscoll.)

Sgt. James Driscoll watches as the Beldon Avenue suspect is transported from the scene. Police officers were breathing sighs of relief while a group of neighbors and onlookers swarm around the patrol car to satisfy their curiosity. (Courtesy of James Driscoll.)

From left to right, Sgt. Casmir Chorazy and patrolmen John Ludgate and Frank Webber lead a suspect from his Catawba Street home after a violent domestic assault, which left the man's wife clinging to life on June 17, 1948. Shortly after 6:00 that morning, the man argued with his wife before striking her in the head with a 15-inch iron bar, fracturing her skull. It was initially believed that the victim would not survive. She did in fact recover. (Courtesy of Syracuse Police Archives.)

This group of meter maids was hired April 25, 1955, to address parking violations without taking police officers away from more pressing issues. In addition to those duties, when budgetary constraints necessitated cutbacks in creek patrol staffing, the meter maids took on some of the patrol duties of the creek patrolmen. (Courtesy of Syracuse Police Archives.)

Patrolmen Arthur Peck (left) and Paul Serban (right) investigate a fatal automobile accident in 1955. (Courtesy of Syracuse Police Archives.)

Patrolmen John Dillon (center) and Paul Callahan (right) interview the driver of a Sunshine Biscuit Company truck who reported having been struck over the head and robbed in May 1955. Their investigation determined that the driver himself had stolen the money belonging to his employer. After having been a popular first deputy chief of the department, John C. Dillon later served many years as sheriff of Onondaga County. The building housing the police department is now named after Dillon. (Courtesy of Syracuse Police Archives.)

Patrolmen Donald Shea and John Leahey interview one of several men in an abandoned building in the 1200 block of East Washington Street at 2:15 a.m. on September 16, 1949. They, along with several other officers, had been sent there to investigate a fight. Instead, they found a dozen men drinking "sneaky Pete." The officers confiscated a couple knives, arrested one of the men, and sent the others away for the night. (Courtesy of Syracuse Police Archives.)

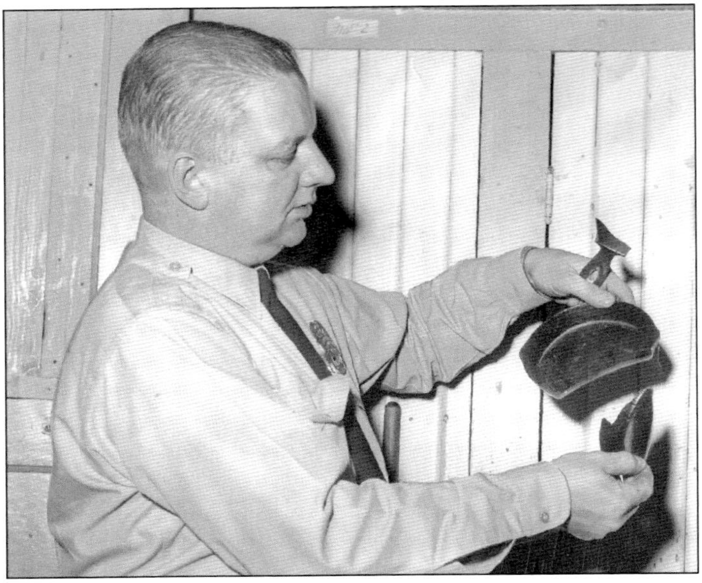

Sgt. Michael Czerniel was assigned as property clerk when he displayed this shattered frying pan. The pan was evidence in the murder of a landlady at 315 University Avenue that occurred on November 21, 1962. The crime was committed by two unemployed laborers, one with the nickname "Big Knife," who had struck the victim in the head at least 14 times, fracturing her skull and killing her. The blows were so forceful that the pan shattered. (Courtesy of the family of Michael Czerneil.)

In 1959, police raided several businesses in the city. They confiscated illegal slot and pinball machines from the Caravan Restaurant, Archie's Diner, and Joe Bell Games. The machines were held as evidence until the cases were disposed of and the Police Court ordered their destruction. The machines met their fate with a sledgehammer swung by Sgt. Michael Czerniel in this photograph taken March 23, 1960. (Courtesy of the family of Michael Czerneil.)

This cornerman is taking time out to provide directions to a driver. Their easily recognizable white hats and regular presence on their corners made these officers readily accessible to motorists and pedestrians alike. This 1963 picture was taken on West Genesee Street just outside the police station. (Courtesy of Syracuse Police Archives.)

Members of the Traffic Division lined up in Clinton Square for this 1963 photograph. In addition to the motorcycle patrolmen and the accident investigation officers, these cornermen were deployed throughout the downtown area. Nearly every main intersection in the downtown area had its own cornerman assigned to it. They were expected to direct traffic and ensure that it flowed smoothly. (Courtesy of Syracuse Police Archives.)

East Genesee Street and Forman Avenue became a flashpoint when racial tensions boiled over in August 1967. These police officers formed at Forman Park to move up Genesee Street and restore order. Several officers were injured when rocks and bottles rained down on them and tensions escalated as gunfire rang out from a rooftop near South Crouse Avenue. (Courtesy of family of Charles DelCostello.)

These police officers, armed with shotguns and tear gas guns, were assigned to three four-man patrol cars to respond to trouble. Nameplates were not standard on uniforms, but officers were directed to remove their badges. From left to right are (kneeling) Claude Richer, Carl Hoyt, Robert Casson, Sgt. Michael Krisak, William O'Hearn, and William Phelps; (standing) Richard Haumann, William Thomas, Eugene Haumann, Wayne Dreher, Richard Schoff, and Michael Chevcheck. (Courtesy of Richard Haumann.)

Rookie police officers Edward Sessler (left) and Peter McLaren (right) participated in a recruiting photo shoot in the 300 block of South Salina Street in August 1965. It was to feature the use of current technology so McLaren was pictured using a walkie-talkie while Sessler recorded the information. Interestingly, the device was actually a transistor radio with a coat hanger fashioned to look like antenna because portables would not be standard issue for nearly a decade. (Courtesy of Edward Sessler.)

This undated photograph shows two unidentified officers responding to a situation at Three Sisters dress store in the 300 block of South Salina Street in the late 1960s. Until shortly after that, the downtown area was the primary commercial district in Onondaga County. Shoppers flocked to clothing and department stores like Chappell's, Edwards, Grants, Witherill's, and Wells and Coverly. Many of the store windows featured animated Christmas displays that rivaled New York City. (Courtesy of Syracuse Police Archives.)

At one time, the police department used an area at the end of Split Rock Road in the town of Camillus for firearms training and qualifications. The area was on the outskirts of where the DuPont Powder Company explosion occurred in 1918. Ronald Arroway is seen training with a Thompson submachine gun at Split Rock on April 29, 1960. Surrounding him are, from left to right, unidentified, Henry Chanley, Robert Mangan, Hector Hayes, and George Dwyer. (Courtesy of Henry Chanley.)

Policeman Edward Uhlig is seen in this picture conducting an ABC inspection at the Del Rio. The bar, which was known for prostitution and other problems, was located in the 100 block of West Onondaga Street. By the early 1970s, the Del Rio was closed for violations of the Alcoholic Beverage Control Act. Inspections such as this contributed to its closing. (Courtesy of Edward Uhlig.)

In the early 1970s, members of the Crime Control Team provided these two bicycles as prizes for an arts-and-crafts contest. The contest was open to children from the Bishop Foery Foundation Center, PEACE Inc., and the Southwest Center. From left to right are Sgt. James Dwyer, police officer Charles DelCostello, and Lt. Michael Byrnes. (Courtesy of family of Charles DelCostello.)

Police officer Otis Thompson (left) discusses conditions on his beat with Sgt. William Nurk (right). Officer Thompson began as a creek patrolman. They were responsible for ensuring public safety along the Onondaga Creek. They manned a series of watch towers at various points along the creek and initially they were part of the Department of Public Works rather than the police department. (Courtesy of Syracuse Police Archives.)

Sgt. Glen Phelps (left) with Ulf and police officer Paul Hudson (right) with Jake pose in front of the Public Safety Building following a graduation ceremony. They became the first Syracuse Police K-9 Unit on March 10, 1987. (Courtesy of Paul Hudson.)

These robbery suspects were stopped on Route 81 in the city of Syracuse. They obviously do not recognize any inexperience on the part of rookie canine Jake. Under Jake's watchful eye, they are very willing to do exactly as directed. (Courtesy of Paul Hudson.)

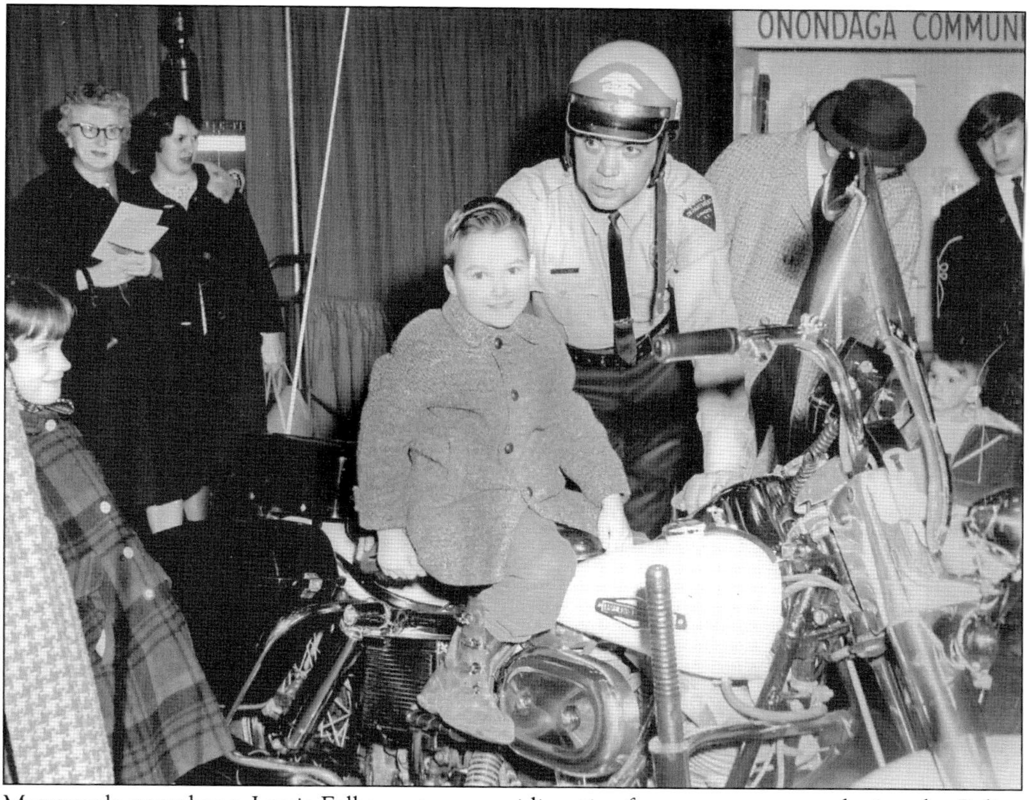

Motorcycle patrolman Lewis Felber gets some riding tips from a young man during the Police Night festivities held at the Onondaga County War Memorial on March 12, 1969. (Courtesy of Syracuse Police Archives.)

Officer Friendly (police officer Charles DelCostello) holds court with a group of young Syracusans in 1974. DelCostello had received the WHEN 5 Gold Badge award for his community relations efforts with the Officer Friendly program, his civic involvement, and his overall performance as a police officer. (Courtesy of the family of Charles DelCostello.)

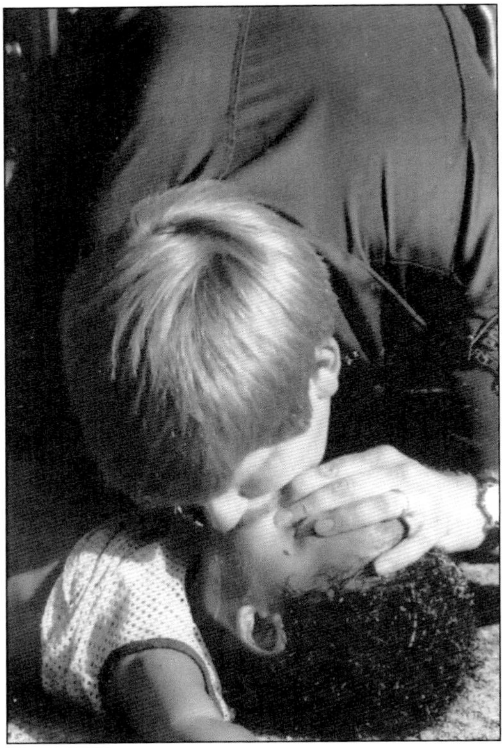

Police officer Paul Hudson, of the department's Emergency Services Unit, revives a two-year-old child after being rescued from Onondaga Creek on July 17, 1979. The toddler was facedown in the water, unconscious, and not breathing when police officer Walter Platt pulled him from a two-feet-deep section of the creek. The child had been thrown from a bridge into the water 20 feet below by an 11-year-old neighbor. (Courtesy of Paul Hudson.)

In yet another rescue from "Killer Creek," Emergency Services police officer Paul Hudson pulls this man from the water of Onondaga Creek. The man had originally contemplated taking his life but reconsidered once he was in the water. (Courtesy of Paul Hudson.)

Seven

LINE OF DUTY DEATHS

A total of 10 police officers have been killed in the line of duty. James Harvey was shot in 1893. Ernest Griffin was killed by a hit-and-run driver in 1921. Pierson Near was shot in 1923. George Caldwell was killed in a motorcycle collision in 1928. James Hannon died after being shot in 1929. Michael English was killed in a motorcycle crash in 1935. John Jarmacz fell from a patrol wagon in 1947. James Considine was killed by a hit-and-run driver, and Mercer Weiskotten was killed in a motorcycle crash in 1954. Wallie Howard was shot in 1990. (Courtesy of Syracuse Police Archives.)

Det. James Harvey was walking burglary suspects Lucius and Charles Wilson through the Bastable Block on July 31, 1893. When they were within sight of the police station, one of the brothers struck Harvey over the head with a revolver. The second one drew his own revolver and shot the detective in the head. Lucius was chased down and captured by citizens and officers at the time of the crime. Charles, however, was able to escape, and a multistate manhunt was launched. Following his capture, both men were tried and convicted. Lucius was executed the following April. Charles lost his sanity while he was in prison and was eventually released. The above display was constructed shortly after Harvey's murder. It contains the revolvers and ammunition taken from the Wilsons when they were arrested, and it remains in the possession of the police department today. (Courtesy of Syracuse Police Archives.)

Lucius Wilson was executed at Auburn Prison for the murder of Det. James Harvey. Before the murder, he had been a member of the notorious Marion Hedgepeth gang of train robbers, and he and other members of the gang had robbed the Glendale train outside of Kansas City. At the time of his arrest in Syracuse, Wilson was the only gang member left who had not been captured or killed. (Courtesy of Syracuse Police Archives.)

On July 10, 1928, patrolman George Caldwell pursued a speeding offender. As he reached Lodi and Court Streets, a truck turned into the path of his police motorcycle. George Caldwell swerved to miss the truck but struck another vehicle. Patrolman John Forsythe is pictured at left as he displays the motorcycle on which Caldwell was killed. (Courtesy of Mark Forsythe.)

Patrolman Jim Hannon was walking a beat on May 1, 1929, when he discovered a burglary in progress at Walker's Pharmacy. He called for assistance from the nearest call box and returned to the store in time to apprehend a suspect as he exited. A second suspect inside the building shot Hannon. Hannon recorded the license number of his fleeing assailant's getaway car, but Hannon died 43 days later. (Courtesy of Syracuse Police Archives.)

On April 7, 1954, patrolman James M. Considine (far left) was directing traffic at a fire scene on Hiawatha Boulevard. With his view obstructed by smoke, a drunk driver ran over patrolman Considine. The driver then left the scene and proceeded to a nearby saloon to calm his nerves. He was apprehended when people there reported him. (Courtesy of Syracuse Police Archives.)

Mercer Weiskotten was chasing a speeding vehicle at 8:50 p.m. on September 23, 1954. Another vehicle failed to yield to the emergency vehicle, and patrolman Weiskotten died of head injuries two hours later. (Courtesy of Syracuse Police Archives.)

Investigator Wallie Howard Jr. was shot and killed in the line of duty on October 30, 1990. He was working undercover when he attempted to make a drug buy in the parking lot of Mario's Big M at South Salina Street and East Brighton Avenue. The suspects, however, had robbery in mind, and investigator Howard was shot as he sat in his car. He was able to shoot and wound one suspect but later lost his fight for life at the hospital. (Courtesy of Syracuse Police Archives.)

Law enforcement personnel from city, county, state, and federal agencies raced to the scene from throughout the county when the call, "Signal 92, officer down, officer shot," pierced the otherwise mundane radio traffic. They put aside their personal emotions and went to work, taking all suspects into custody and conducting an investigation that would result in prison sentences for all of them. Conferring at the scene are, from left to right, Lt. Robert Driscoll and police officers Douglas Fox and Daniel Forkhamer. (Courtesy of the *Post Standard*.)

Hundreds of Syracuse police officers escort investigator Howard's body to Assumption Church on North Salina Street. Thousands of other law enforcement personnel from all over the country met in Syracuse to honor the life and service of Wallie Howard Jr. (Courtesy of the *Post Standard*.)

Like so many others, police recruit Dawn Villa Daley struggled to contain normal human emotions. Police chief Leigh Hunt spoke from the podium of a church packed shoulder to shoulder with family members and police officers. His voice cracked as he gazed at a tearful little boy in the front row and said, "I think it's important that you know little Wallie the third, I see you out there crying, that grown men cry too." (Courtesy of the *Post Standard*.)